Canadian Rockies Travel Guide

Explore Banff and Jasper, Hidden Trails, Iconic Landmarks, and Unique Local Experiences.

Miles B. Carter

All rights reserved. No part of this publication may be reproduced, distributed, or transmitted in any form or by any means, including photocopying, recording, or other electronic or mechanical methods, without the prior written permission of the publisher, except in the case of brief quotations embodied in critical reviews and certain other noncommercial uses permitted by copyright law.

Copyright ©Miles B. Carter, 2024.

Table of Content.

1. Introduction to Banff and Jasper National Parks

    - Overview of the Parks and What Makes Them Unique

    - History and Significance

    - Essential Things to Know Before You Go

2. When to Visit: Best Times for Every Adventure

    - Seasonal Highlights: Summer vs. Winter

    - Weather Considerations and Wildlife Sightings

    - Special Events and Festivals

3. How to Get There: Travel and Transportation

    - Nearest Airports and Travel Routes

    - Renting a Car vs. Public Transportation

    - Tips for the Icefields Parkway Drive

4. Where to Stay: Accommodation Options for Every Budget

    - Campgrounds, Lodges, and Hotels

    - Unique Stays: From Cozy Cabins to Luxury Resorts

    - Booking Tips and Availability

5. What to Pack: Gear and Essentials for Every Season

   - Summer Hiking and Camping Gear

   - Winter Sports Equipment and Warm Clothing

   - First Aid, Navigation Tools, and Safety Tips

6. Must-See Sights in Banff National Park

   - Iconic Landmarks: Lake Louise, Moraine Lake, and Banff Gondola

   - Scenic Drives and Photo Spots

   - Hidden Gems and Less Crowded Areas

7. Top Attractions in Jasper National Park

   - Athabasca Falls, Maligne Canyon, and Spirit Island

   - Wildlife Viewing: Where and When to Spot Animals

   - Adventure Activities: Canoeing, Horseback Riding, and More

8. Outdoor Adventures: Hiking, Biking, and More..

   - Best Hiking Trails for All Levels in Both Parks

   - Cycling Routes, Scenic Walks, and Family-Friendly Paths

   - Adventure Sports: Climbing, Kayaking, and Rafting

9. Wildlife and Nature: Flora and Fauna to Look Out.

   - Bears, Elk, Moose, and More: Responsible Wildlife Viewing

   - Nature Preservation and Conservation Efforts

   - Guided Tours and Nature Walks

10. Dining in the Rockies: Best Food and Drink Options

    - Local Restaurants and Cafés in Banff and Jasper

    - Picnic Spots and Where to Enjoy Local Cuisine

    - Sustainable and Eco-Friendly Dining

11. Safety Tips for Outdoor Exploration

    - Staying Safe Around Wildlife

    - Navigating Trails and Avoiding Hazards

    - Emergency Contacts and Safety Resources

12. Traveling with your kids

Most visit sports with family and kids

Kids friendly accommodations

Budget friendly restaurants

Traveling with your pets

13. Photography Tips: Capturing the Beauty of the Parks

   - Best Times for Golden Hour Photography

   - Key Locations for Stunning Photos

   - Photography Etiquette in Nature

14. Final Tips for a Memorable Trip

   - Eco-Friendly Travel Practices and Leave No Trace

   - Insider Tips from Locals and Park Rangers

     - Acknowledgement
     - Maps & Travel Planners

Chapter 1

Introduction to Banff and Jasper National Parks

Have you ever imagined stepping into a postcard?

That's what it feels like to visit Banff and Jasper National Parks. These twin jewels of the Canadian Rockies are a wonderland of soaring peaks, turquoise lakes, and abundant wildlife. But they're more than just a pretty picture. These parks have a rich history and distinct personalities that make them truly unique. So, buckle up, grab your hiking boots, and let's embark on a journey through time and nature!

A Tale of Two Parks: From Hot Springs to Mountain Majesty

Banff National Park, established in 1885, is Canada's oldest national park. It all began with the discovery of natural hot springs, sparking a debate over ownership and ultimately leading to the protection of this incredible landscape. Originally a modest reserve around the Cave and Basin Hot Springs, Banff quickly grew to encompass breathtaking scenery, including Lake Louise and the iconic Valley of the Ten Peaks.

Jasper National Park, established in 1907, is the wilder, larger sibling of Banff. While Banff was born from a desire to protect a natural wonder, Jasper's origins lie in the railway. As the Grand Trunk Pacific Railway carved its way through the wilderness, the government saw the potential for a mountain paradise to rival Banff.

Landscapes Painted by Nature's Hand

While both parks share the rugged beauty of the Canadian Rockies, they each possess a unique character.

Banff is known for its dramatic contrasts: the glacial blues of Lake Louise against the towering Victoria Glacier, the vibrant turquoise of Moraine Lake nestled amongst the Valley of the Ten Peaks. It's a land of accessible beauty, with well-maintained trails and iconic viewpoints that draw visitors from around the globe.

Jasper, on the other hand, is a realm of untamed wilderness. Here, the mountains seem to stretch forever, their peaks shrouded in mist and mystery. The Athabasca Glacier, a colossal tongue of ice flowing from the Columbia Icefield, is a testament to the raw power of nature. Jasper's vastness offers a sense of solitude and adventure that's harder to find in its more popular counterpart.

Where the Wild Things Roam

Both parks are teeming with wildlife, but their inhabitants have adapted to the nuances of their environments.

In Banff, you might spot a majestic elk grazing in a meadow, a black bear foraging for berries, or a playful marmot scampering across a trail. Keep your eyes peeled for bighorn sheep scaling the cliffs and soaring eagles circling overhead.

Jasper, with its vast wilderness, is home to a greater diversity of creatures. Here, you have a better chance of encountering elusive animals like the woodland caribou, the lynx, and even the mighty grizzly bear. Remember to keep a safe distance and respect their wild home.

Planning Your Banff and Jasper Adventure.

Before you lace up your hiking boots and hit the trails, there are a few essential things to know about visiting Banff and Jasper National Parks. Think of this as your pre-trip briefing, ensuring a smooth and enjoyable experience in these mountain wonderlands.

Park Passes: Your Ticket to Explore

To enter Banff and Jasper National Parks, you'll need a valid park pass. Consider these options:

- Daily Pass: Perfect for short visits, this pass grants you access for one day.

- Discovery Pass: If you plan to explore multiple national parks in Canada, the Discovery Pass is your best bet. It provides unlimited admission for a full year to all Parks Canada locations.

Tip: Purchase your pass online in advance to save time at the park gates. You can also buy them at park entrance gates and visitor centers.

Entry Fees: A Small Price for Unspoiled Beauty

While the parks themselves are priceless, there are nominal entry fees to help maintain these natural treasures. Fees vary depending on age and whether you're traveling solo or as a family. Children under 17 enter for free – a great incentive for a family adventure!

Good to Know: Your park pass covers your entry fee, so you won't have to pay twice.

Respecting the Wild: Visitor Guidelines

Banff and Jasper are home to diverse ecosystems and wildlife. To ensure their protection and your safety, please follow these guidelines:

- Stay on marked trails: This helps prevent erosion and minimizes disturbance to wildlife habitats.

- Keep a safe distance from wildlife: Admire these creatures from afar, using binoculars or a telephoto lens. Feeding or approaching wildlife is strictly prohibited and can be dangerous.

- Pack out everything you pack in: Leave no trace of your visit. Dispose of trash properly and recycle whenever possible.

- Be bear aware: Carry bear spray and know how to use it. Store food and scented items securely to avoid attracting bears.

- Respect fire regulations: Fires are only permitted in designated fire pits. Check for fire bans before you go.

Chapter 2.

The Best Time to Explore Banff and Jasper.

Banff and Jasper National Parks are stunning year-round, but each season offers a unique experience. Whether you're a sun-seeking hiker, a snowshoeing enthusiast, or a wildlife-spotting pro, there's a perfect time to visit these mountain playgrounds.

Summer (June - August): Sunshine and Summits

What to Expect: Long sunny days, wildflowers bursting with color, and glacier-fed lakes shimmering in the sunlight. This is peak season, so expect crowds and book accommodations well in advance.

What to Do:

- Hiking: Hit the trails! From leisurely lakeside strolls to challenging mountain climbs, there's a hike for every level. Popular trails include the Plain of Six Glaciers Trail (Lake Louise), Johnston Canyon (Banff), and the Valley of the Five Lakes (Jasper).

- Canoeing and Kayaking: Paddle across turquoise waters, surrounded by mountain vistas. Rent canoes or kayaks at Lake Louise, Moraine Lake, or Maligne Lake.

- Wildlife Viewing: Animals are most active in summer. Join a guided tour or explore on your own, keeping an eye out for elk, deer, bears, and marmots.

- Scenic Drives: Cruise along the Icefields Parkway, stopping at viewpoints like Bow Lake and Peyto Lake for breathtaking panoramas.

What to Wear: Pack layers for warm days and cool evenings. Bring hiking boots, a hat, sunscreen, and a rain jacket.

Where to Rent Gear: You'll find outdoor gear rentals in Banff, Lake Louise, and Jasper town. Check out Wilson Mountain Sports, Snowtips-Bactrax, and Totem Ski Shop.

Fall (September - October): Golden Hues and Crisp Air

What to Expect: The crowds thin out, the air turns crisp, and the larch trees transform into a golden spectacle. This is a photographer's dream!

What to Do:

- Larch Tree Hiking: Witness the magic of the larch trees turning gold. Popular larch hikes include Larch Valley (Moraine Lake) and Sentinel Pass (Lake Louise).

- Wildlife Viewing: Fall is mating season for elk, so you might hear their bugling calls echoing through the valleys. Keep an eye out for bears preparing for hibernation.

- Scenic Drives: The Icefields Parkway is even more stunning in fall, with golden larches contrasting against the turquoise lakes and snow-capped peaks.

What to Wear: Pack layers for cool days and chilly evenings. Bring a warm jacket, gloves, a hat, and sturdy hiking boots.

Where to Rent Gear: The same rental shops from summer will have you covered for your fall adventures.

Winter (November - April): A Winter Wonderland

What to Expect: Snow blankets the landscape, transforming the parks into a winter wonderland. This is the time for snowy adventures and cozy evenings by the fire.

What to Do:

- Skiing and Snowboarding: Hit the slopes at Lake Louise Ski Resort, Sunshine Village, or Marmot Basin.

- Snowshoeing and Cross-Country Skiing: Explore the trails at your own pace, surrounded by snowy forests and frozen lakes. Rent snowshoes or skis in Banff, Lake Louise, or Jasper.

- Ice Skating: Glide across the frozen surface of Lake Louise or Two Jack Lake.

- Soaking in Hot Springs: Warm up in the Banff Upper Hot Springs after a day of winter activities.

What to Wear: Bundle up! Pack warm layers, including a waterproof jacket, snow pants, a hat, gloves, and warm socks.

Where to Rent Gear: Ski resorts offer rentals, as do shops in town like Wilson Mountain Sports and Snowtips-Bactrax.

Spring (May - June): Awakening and Adventure

What to Expect: The snow begins to melt, revealing vibrant wildflowers and rushing waterfalls. Wildlife emerges from hibernation, and the parks come alive with new life.

What to Do:

- Hiking: Lower elevation trails are usually accessible in spring. Enjoy the wildflowers and waterfalls without the summer crowds.

- Wildlife Viewing: Spot bears emerging from hibernation, newborn animals, and migratory birds returning to the parks.

- Whitewater Rafting: Experience the thrill of rafting on the Athabasca River as the snowmelt swells the rapids.

What to Wear: Pack layers for unpredictable weather. Bring a waterproof jacket, hiking boots, and a warm sweater.

Where to Rent Gear: Rafting companies provide all necessary equipment. For hiking gear, check out the usual suspects in Banff and Jasper.

Wildlife and Events Throughout the Year

Banff and Jasper are dynamic places, constantly changing with the seasons. Wildlife activity shifts, landscapes transform, and festivals bring vibrant energy to the towns. Here's a glimpse into how nature and culture intertwine throughout the year:

Wildlife Watching: Seasonal Shifts

Spring (May-June):

- Bears: Emerge from hibernation, often seen with cubs.
- Elk: Calves are born, adding to the herds.
- Birds: Migratory birds return, filling the air with song.

Summer (June-August):

- All Wildlife: Most active due to abundant food and warm weather.
- Elk: Gather in meadows for mating season, with bulls bugling.

Fall (September-October):

- Bears: Actively foraging for food before hibernation.
- Elk: Rutting season continues, with dramatic displays.

Winter (November-April):

- Most Wildlife: Less active, some hibernate or migrate.

- Wolves: May be seen hunting in packs.

Best Time to Spot:

- Bears: Spring and Fall (dawn and dusk)
- Elk: Summer and Fall (early morning and evening)

Festivals and Events: A Year of Celebration

Event	Time of Year	Description	Booking Tips
Lake Louise Ski Resort Winterstart Festival	November	Kick off the ski season with live music, parties, and early season skiing.	Book accommodations and lift tickets in advance.
Christmas in Banff & Lake Louise	December	Enjoy festive decorations, carol singing, and holiday markets.	Book accommodations and activities early.
Ice Magic Festival	January	Marvel at ice sculptures	Purchase tickets online in advance.

(Lake Louise)		created by world-renowned artists.	
SnowDays (Banff & Lake Louise)	January/February	Celebrate winter with snow sculptures, ice skating, and family-friendly activities.	Check the website for event schedules and activity bookings.
Jasper in January	January	Embrace winter with outdoor activities like ice climbing, fat biking, and snowshoeing.	Book accommodations and activities early.
Dark Sky Festival (Jasper)	October	Explore the wonders of astronomy with	Purchase tickets for events and workshops in advance.

| | | stargazing, presentations, and workshops. | |

Chapter 3

How to Get There: Travel and Transportation.

Okay, explorers, now that you're dreaming of turquoise lakes and mountain peaks, let's map out your route to Banff and Jasper National Parks. Whether you prefer the freedom of the open road, the scenic comfort of a train, or the convenience of a bus, there are options to suit every traveler.

By Air: Taking Flight to Mountain Majesty

The closest major airport to Banff National Park is Calgary International Airport (YYC), located about 130 km (80 miles) east of Banff townsite. For Jasper National Park, the closest airport is Edmonton International Airport (YEG), approximately 360 km (225 miles) east of Jasper townsite.

From Calgary Airport to Banff:

- Shuttle Bus: Several shuttle services, like Brewster Express and Banff Airporter, offer convenient transfers between the airport and Banff. You can book your shuttle in advance online or at the airport.

- Rental Car: Pick up a rental car at the airport and enjoy the scenic drive to Banff. This option gives you flexibility to explore at your own pace.

- Taxi: Taxis are available at the airport, but this is the most expensive option.

From Edmonton Airport to Jasper:

- Sundog Tours: Offers a shuttle service between Edmonton Airport and Jasper, with stunning scenery along the Icefields Parkway.

- Rental Car: Rent a car at the airport and embark on a scenic road trip to Jasper. Be sure to factor in extra time for stops along the Icefields Parkway.

By Road: Cruising the Scenic Routes

Driving to Banff:

- Trans-Canada Highway (Highway 1): This major highway connects Calgary to Banff. The drive is approximately 1.5 hours and offers stunning views of the foothills and mountains.

- Bow Valley Parkway (Highway 1A): This scenic alternative to the Trans-Canada Highway runs parallel to the Bow River and offers opportunities for wildlife viewing.

Driving to Jasper:

- Icefields Parkway (Highway 93): This iconic highway connects Lake Louise to Jasper, winding through breathtaking mountain scenery, glaciers, and turquoise lakes. Allow at least 4-5 hours for the drive, with extra time for stops and photo opportunities.

Important Note: Winter driving conditions can be challenging in the Rockies. Ensure your vehicle is equipped with winter tires and be prepared for snow and ice.

By Rail: A Journey Through Time

While there's no direct train service to Banff, you can take the Rocky Mountaineer to Jasper. This luxury train offers a scenic journey through the Canadian Rockies, with breathtaking views and onboard amenities.

From Jasper to Banff:

- Sundog Tours: Offers a shuttle service between Jasper and Banff, allowing you to combine the train journey with a scenic road trip.

By Bus: Affordable and Convenient

Sundog Tours and Brewster Express offer bus services between Banff and Jasper, with stops at key attractions along the Icefields Parkway. This is a great option for budget-conscious travelers who want to enjoy the scenery without driving.

Renting a Car vs. Public Transportation.

Getting around Banff and Jasper National Parks is part of the adventure. But with options like rental cars and public transportation, which one is right for you? Let's weigh the pros and cons, and then I'll share some insider tips for navigating the legendary Icefields Parkway.

Rental Cars: Freedom on Four Wheels

Advantages:

- Flexibility: Go where you want, when you want. No schedules to follow, no waiting for buses.

- Explore at Your Own Pace: Stop at scenic viewpoints, hidden trails, and charming towns along the way.

- Convenience: Carry your gear, snacks, and souvenirs with ease.

- Reach Remote Areas: Access trailheads, lakes, and viewpoints that may not be served by public transportation.

Disadvantages:

- Cost: Rental fees, gas, parking, and potential for traffic tickets can add up.

- Parking Challenges: Finding parking at popular attractions can be tricky, especially during peak season.

- Driving Stress: Navigating unfamiliar roads, mountain passes, and wildlife can be stressful for some drivers.
- Environmental Impact: Contributes to carbon emissions.

Rental Companies:

- Major Agencies: Hertz, Avis, Budget, Enterprise (available at Calgary and Edmonton airports)
- Local Companies: Banff Car and Truck Rentals, Pursuit Banff Jasper Collection (offers a variety of vehicles, including campervans)
- Websites: Kayak, Expedia, Rentalcars.com (compare prices and book online)

Public Transportation: Sit Back and Enjoy the Ride

Advantages:

- Relax and Enjoy the Scenery: Let someone else do the driving while you soak in the views.
- Cost-Effective: Often cheaper than renting a car, especially for solo travelers or couples.
- Environmentally Friendly: Reduces carbon footprint.
- Stress-Free: Avoid the hassle of driving and parking.

Disadvantages:

- Limited Flexibility: Restricted to bus schedules and routes.
- Less Access to Remote Areas: May not reach all trailheads and viewpoints.

- Crowds: Buses can get crowded, especially during peak season.

Public Transportation Options:

- Brewster Express: Offers shuttle services between Calgary Airport, Banff, Lake Louise, and Jasper.

- Sundog Tours: Provides shuttles between Edmonton Airport, Jasper, and Banff, as well as tours along the Icefields Parkway.

- Roam Transit: Local bus service within Banff National Park.

Conquering the Icefields Parkway: A Driver's Guide

The Icefields Parkway (Highway 93) is a 232 km (144 mile) ribbon of asphalt that winds through the heart of the Canadian Rockies, connecting Lake Louise to Jasper. It's a journey through a landscape of towering peaks, glaciers, turquoise lakes, and waterfalls. Here's how to make the most of this iconic drive:

Must-See Stops:

- Lake Louise: A glacial lake with iconic views of Victoria Glacier and the Fairmont Chateau Lake Louise.

- Moraine Lake: Nestled in the Valley of the Ten Peaks, this turquoise gem is a photographer's dream.

- Bow Lake: The largest lake in Banff National Park, offering stunning reflections of the surrounding mountains.

- Peyto Lake: Known for its distinctive wolf-shaped outline and vibrant turquoise color.

- Columbia Icefield: A massive icefield where you can walk on the Athabasca Glacier or take an Ice Explorer tour.
- Athabasca Falls: A powerful waterfall cascading through a narrow gorge.
- Sunwapta Falls: A series of cascading waterfalls surrounded by lush forest.

Driving Tips:

- Allow Ample Time: The drive takes at least 4-5 hours, but factor in extra time for stops, photos, and potential wildlife encounters.
- Fill Up Your Tank: Gas stations are limited along the Parkway.
- Be Prepared for Weather Changes: Mountain weather can be unpredictable, so pack layers and be ready for rain, snow, or shine.
- Watch for Wildlife: Animals like elk, deer, and bears often cross the road. Drive slowly and be alert.
- Obey Speed Limits: Speed limits are strictly enforced, and fines are hefty.
- Pull Over for Photos: Numerous pullouts offer safe and scenic spots for photos.
- Pack Snacks and Water: Limited food options are available along the way.
- Download Offline Maps: Cell service can be spotty, so download offline maps or bring a paper map.

Whether you choose to rent a car or hop on a bus, the journey through Banff and Jasper National Parks is an unforgettable experience. So, buckle up, embrace the adventure, and get ready to be amazed by the Canadian Rockies.

Chapter 4

Accommodation Options for Every Budget.

Banff and Jasper National Parks offer a diverse range of accommodations to suit every budget and taste. Whether you crave the luxury of a mountain lodge, the rustic charm of a cabin, or the camaraderie of a hostel, you'll find the perfect place to rest your head after a day of adventure.

Luxury Lodges: Indulge in Mountain Grandeur

- **Fairmont Banff Springs:** (405 Spray Ave, Banff, AB T1L 1J4) This iconic "Castle in the Rockies" offers opulent rooms, fine dining, a world-class spa, and breathtaking views.

- **Fairmont Chateau Lake Louise:** (111 Lake Louise Dr, Lake Louise, AB T0L 1E0) Nestled on the shores of Lake Louise, this grand hotel boasts elegant rooms, gourmet restaurants, and unparalleled access to the lake and surrounding trails.

- **Post Hotel & Spa:** (200 Pipestone Rd, Lake Louise, AB T0L 1E0) This Relais & Châteaux property offers a luxurious escape with cozy rooms, a renowned wine cellar, and a soothing spa.

- **Fairmont Jasper Park Lodge:** (1 Old Lodge Rd, Jasper, AB T0E 1E0) Spread across 700 acres, this sprawling resort features charming cabins, a championship golf course, and a serene lakeside setting.

Unique Activities:

- **Fairmont Banff Springs:** Afternoon tea in the Rundle Lounge, a historical tour of the hotel, and a soak in the mineral pool.

- **Fairmont Chateau Lake Louise:** Canoeing on Lake Louise, ice skating in winter, and a guided hike to the Plain of Six Glaciers.

- **Post Hotel & Spa:** Wine tasting in the cellar, a relaxing massage in the spa, and a gourmet dinner at the renowned Sir Norman Lounge.

- **Fairmont Jasper Park Lodge:** Golfing on the championship course, horseback riding through the forest, and stargazing on the shores of Lac Beauvert.

Mid-Range Comfort: Cozy Cabins and Mountain Inns

- **Buffalo Mountain Lodge:** (Tunnel Mountain Rd, Banff, AB T1L 1H8) This charming lodge offers rustic-chic cabins with fireplaces, a relaxing outdoor hot tub, and a convenient location near downtown Banff.

- **Moose Hotel & Suites:** (345 Banff Ave, Banff, AB T1L 1H8) This modern hotel features spacious suites with kitchenettes, a rooftop hot tub with mountain views, and a lively après-ski atmosphere.

- **Mount Robson Inn:** (800 Connaught Dr, Jasper, AB T0E 1E0) This family-friendly inn offers comfortable rooms, a heated indoor pool, and a convenient location near Jasper's shops and restaurants.

- **Pyramid Lake Resort:** (Pyramid Lake Rd, Jasper, AB T0E 1E0) Nestled on the shores of Pyramid Lake, this resort offers cozy cabins with fireplaces, a restaurant with stunning lake views, and opportunities for canoeing and kayaking.

Unique Activities:

- **Buffalo Mountain Lodge:** Relaxing by the outdoor fireplace, enjoying a soak in the hot tub, and exploring nearby hiking trails.

- **Moose Hotel & Suites:** Enjoying a drink on the rooftop patio with mountain views, playing a game of pool in the games room, and taking a dip in the outdoor hot tub.

- **Mount Robson Inn:** Exploring Jasper townsite on foot, taking a dip in the heated pool, and enjoying a family-friendly movie night in the lounge.

- **Pyramid Lake Resort:** Canoeing or kayaking on Pyramid Lake, hiking to Pyramid Mountain for panoramic views, and enjoying a romantic dinner with lake views.

Budget-Friendly Adventures: Camping and Hostels

- **Tunnel Mountain Village II Campground:** (Tunnel Mountain Rd, Banff, AB T1L 1K8) This popular campground offers campsites with fire pits, picnic tables, and stunning views of the surrounding mountains.

- **Wapiti Campground:** (Icefields Pkwy, Jasper, AB T0E 1E0) Located along the Icefields Parkway, this campground offers a peaceful escape with campsites nestled among the trees.

- **HI Banff Alpine Centre:** (Tunnel Mountain Rd, Banff, AB T1L 1H5) This hostel offers affordable dorm rooms and private rooms, a communal kitchen, and a social atmosphere.

- **HI Jasper:** (912 Connaught Dr, Jasper, AB T0E 1E0) This hostel features cozy common areas, a spacious kitchen, and organized activities like hikes and pub crawls.

Unique Activities:

- **Tunnel Mountain Village II Campground:** Roasting marshmallows around a campfire, stargazing under the clear mountain sky, and enjoying a picnic lunch with a view.

- **Wapiti Campground:** Hiking to nearby lakes and waterfalls, exploring the Icefields Parkway, and enjoying the peace and quiet of the wilderness.

- **HI Banff Alpine Centre:** Meeting fellow travelers in the common room, cooking a communal meal in the kitchen, and joining organized hikes and social events.

- **HI Jasper:** Sharing travel stories with other backpackers, exploring Jasper's nightlife scene, and joining a guided hike to a hidden waterfall.

No matter your budget or travel style, you'll find a welcoming place to stay in Banff and Jasper National Parks. So, book your dream accommodation, pack your bags, and get ready for an unforgettable mountain adventure!

Cozy Cabins to Luxury Resorts

When planning your trip to Banff and Jasper National Parks, there's a wide range of accommodations available to fit various budgets and preferences, from luxurious lodges to budget-friendly campgrounds. Here's a breakdown:

Luxury Options

- **Sunshine Mountain Lodge (Banff)**: This lodge is ideal for families or couples looking for a luxury experience. It's a ski-in/ski-out lodge with amenities like a spa, swimming pool, and scheduled family activities like snowshoeing and tobogganing during winter. It offers easy access to Banff's top attractions, and you can even enjoy dinner at one of its on-site restaurants

- **Chateau Elise Mountain Home (Canmore)**: For those wanting an extravagant stay, this multi-million-dollar mountain home offers incredible views, a hot tub, and luxurious stone and wood designs. You're close to hiking trails and ski slopes, making it a perfect spot for adventure (The Broke Backpacker)

Mid-Range Options

- **Mount Robson Inn (Jasper)**: Located near Athabasca Falls, this mid-range hotel offers modern comforts with hot tubs, stylish interiors, and essential amenities like Wi-Fi and coffee makers

- **Jasper Inn & Suites**: A great option for those who want a balance between comfort and affordability. It includes a swimming pool, hot tub, and even a ski wax room during winter (The Wandering Queen)

Budget-Friendly Options

- **Jasper Downtown Hostel**: If you're on a tighter budget, this hostel in the heart of Jasper offers both dormitory and private rooms. Guests have access to shared kitchen and laundry facilities.

- **Banff Beaver Cabins**: These charming cabins offer a cozy experience with amenities like a kitchenette, BBQ area, and Wi-Fi, making them perfect for families or small groups wanting to stay in the heart of Banff

- **Campgrounds**

If you prefer a more immersive nature experience, there are numerous campgrounds in both parks:

- **Wapiti Campground (Jasper)**: Open year-round, it offers electric hookups, hot showers, and fire pits. It's also right along the Athabasca River, providing a serene camping experience.

- **Tunnel Mountain Campground (Banff)**: This site provides overflow camping for those sleeping in vehicles. It's an affordable, no-frills option with easy access to the town of Banff.

Booking Tips

For campgrounds, especially in the summer, it's best to reserve early as they fill up quickly. If you don't have a reservation, arriving early in the morning increases your chances of getting a spot, especially at first-come-first-serve campgrounds like Snaring River in Jasper (Bearfoot Theory).

For hotels and lodges, booking through official websites or popular platforms like Booking.com or Airbnb can help you find the best deals, especially during off-peak seasons (The Broke Backpacker).

Booking Tips and Availability.

To choose the best location to stay in Banff and Jasper National Parks, travelers should consider their itinerary, interests, and proximity to specific activities such as hiking, lake visits, or sightseeing. Here's how you can select the best area to stay, along with booking tips to ensure a smooth trip.

Choosing Accommodation Based on Interests:

- **Hiking Enthusiasts:** If hiking is the focus, you should stay near trailheads or within easy access to popular trails. In **Banff**, staying at locations like **Sunshine Village** or **Tunnel Mountain** gives you quick access to some of the park's best hiking routes. In **Jasper**, look for places near **Whistlers Campground** or **Wapiti Campground**, as these areas are close to iconic trails such as the **Athabasca Glacier** and the **Valley of the Five Lakes**.

- **Lakes and Scenic Views:** For travelers focused on lakes and water activities, accommodations near **Lake Louise** in Banff or **Pyramid Lake** in Jasper would be ideal. These areas offer breathtaking scenery and are close to boat rentals, kayaking, and picnic spots. **Lake Louise** area offers luxury stays at places like the **Fairmont Chateau Lake Louise**, while budget options like the **Lake Louise Overflow Campground** are available for campers.

- **Wildlife Watching:** If spotting wildlife is a priority, stay in more remote areas. In Banff, locations like **Castle Mountain Junction** provide great opportunities to see wildlife. In Jasper, **Pocahontas**

Campground offers a quieter location away from the busier town areas, giving you more chances to see elk, bears, and other animals.

Booking Tips:

1. **Timing**: For peak season (June to August), it's recommended to book 6 to 12 months in advance. Summer is extremely busy, and both campgrounds and hotels fill up quickly. Campgrounds like **Tunnel Mountain** and **Whistlers** allow reservations online, but many sites, especially first-come, first-served campgrounds like **Snaring River**, are highly competitive.

2. **Off-Peak Seasons**: If you're visiting in the shoulder seasons (May or September), you might have more flexibility. For campgrounds, showing up early in the morning increases your chances of snagging a spot without reservations.

3. **Last-Minute Availability**: Even during peak times, some campgrounds in Banff, such as **Tunnel Mountain** and **Two Jack Lake**, occasionally have last-minute openings due to cancellations. It's a good idea to check daily, particularly in the early morning.

4. **Winter Stays**: If you're visiting during the winter, Jasper's **Wapiti Campground** remains open year-round and offers a more peaceful experience with fewer crowds. Hotels and lodges like **Sunshine Mountain Lodge** in Banff also cater to winter visitors looking for ski-in, ski-out accommodations.

Accommodation Based on Itinerary or Interests.

Hiking Enthusiasts:

For those focused on hiking, the key is proximity to popular trailheads.

Banff:

- Staying in **Sunshine Village** or near **Tunnel Mountain Campground** offers direct access to key trails like the **Sulphur Mountain** trail, **Larch Valley**, and **Cory Pass**. These areas provide a range of accommodations from campgrounds to luxury lodges. **Sunshine Mountain Lodge** offers ski-in/ski-out accommodations in winter and proximity to hiking trails in the summer. **Tunnel Mountain Campground** is a great budget-friendly option with access to shuttle services that can take you to nearby trailheads.

- **Jasper**:

Stay near **Whistlers Campground** or **Wapiti Campground** for easy access to the **Athabasca Glacier**, the **Skyline Trail**, and the **Valley of the Five Lakes** trail. **Whistlers Campground**, with over 700 sites, also offers glamping options with **oTENTik tents** for a more comfortable experience. These sites are close to Jasper's main attractions and are ideal for families and hikers alike

Proximity to Lakes and Scenic Views:

If you're looking to enjoy iconic lakes like **Lake Louise** or **Peyto Lake**, staying near these bodies of water provides both stunning views and easy access to outdoor activities such as canoeing and paddleboarding.

- **Banff**:

Consider staying at the luxurious **Fairmont Chateau Lake Louise**, where you'll be right on the shores of **Lake Louise** with easy access to **Moraine Lake** as well. There are also shuttle services that can take you from the overflow camping areas at **Lake Louise Overflow Campground** to the main attractions, which is an economical choice

- **Jasper**:

Pyramid Lake Resort in Jasper offers stunning views and proximity to **Pyramid Lake** and **Patricia Lake**, where you can enjoy boating, fishing, or just taking in the scenery. The resort also provides access to biking trails and hiking routes that surround the lakes.

Wildlife Watching:

Staying in quieter, more remote areas increases the likelihood of encountering wildlife like elk, bears, and wolves.

- **Banff**:

Consider **Castle Mountain Junction** or **Lake Louise Campground**, which are known for their frequent wildlife sightings. Castle Mountain provides a more remote and less crowded setting, perfect for those looking to escape the busy town of Banff

- **Jasper**:

Pocahontas Campground, located further from the town center, is perfect for those who want to stay off the beaten path and enjoy the quieter parts of the park. You'll also have a good chance of spotting wildlife here, as it is less frequented by tourists

Winter Sports and Activities:

For those visiting in winter, both parks offer accommodations that are perfectly situated for skiing, snowshoeing, and other winter activities.

- **Banff**:

The **Sunshine Mountain Lodge** is the only ski-in/ski-out lodge in Banff and offers direct access to skiing at Sunshine Village. In the evenings, families can enjoy scheduled movie nights, while the more adventurous can take part in snowshoe tours,

- **Jasper**:

Wapiti Campground is open year-round, and while camping in winter may not be for everyone, it offers a peaceful alternative to the busy summer months. Winter visitors can enjoy cross-country skiing and ice skating at nearby **Pyramid Lake**

Booking Tips:

Peak Season (June to August):

During the peak summer season, both Banff and Jasper National Parks experience a high volume of visitors. Here's how to secure your accommodations:

- **Book Early**: For hotels and lodges, booking 6 to 12 months in advance is essential. Popular options like the **Fairmont Chateau Lake Louise** and **Sunshine**

Mountain Lodge fill up quickly. If you plan to stay in one of the campgrounds that allow reservations, such as **Whistlers** or **Tunnel Mountain**, aim to secure your spot as soon as reservations open

- **First-Come, First-Served Campgrounds**: If you haven't made a reservation, arrive early in the morning (before 9 a.m.) to secure a spot. This is especially important for campgrounds like **Snaring River** in Jasper or the **Two Jack Lake Campground** in Banff. Be prepared to wait in line and have alternative options in mind.

Off-Peak Season (Spring and Fall):

The shoulder seasons in May and September offer more flexibility. During these months, you can often book accommodations closer to your travel dates without as much competition, and prices tend to be lower.

- **Campgrounds and Lodges**: In Jasper, sites like **Wapiti** and **Pocahontas Campground** remain relatively available, though it's still smart to book a few months ahead to ensure you get your preferred spot

- **Winter Stays**: If you're visiting in winter (November to March), there's less demand for accommodations, though it's still recommended to book a couple of months ahead for lodges like **Sunshine Mountain Lodge** or cabins near **Lake Louise**, which offer ski-in, ski-out access.

Last-Minute Options:

- **Cancellations**: Campgrounds and hotels may have last-minute cancellations, especially in Banff. Check daily for openings, and you might score a site at places like **Tunnel Mountain Campground** or even a room at **The Rundlestone Lodge**.

- **Overflow Camping**: Both parks offer overflow camping for those who don't mind a no-frills experience. **Lake Louise Overflow Campground** and **Snaring River Overflow** provide basic services like restrooms and parking, but they're affordable options when everything else is full.

Chapter 5

What to Pack: Gear and Essentials for Every Season.

When packing for Banff and Jasper National Parks, what you bring with you can make or break your trip. The parks offer vastly different experiences depending on the season, and you'll need to be prepared for each one's specific challenges. Whether you're exploring the parks during the warm summer months or tackling the snow-covered trails in winter, here's a detailed guide on what gear and essentials you should pack.

Summer Packing List (June to September)

Summer in Banff and Jasper is all about hiking, sightseeing, and getting out into nature. However, the weather can be unpredictable, and temperatures can vary greatly throughout the day, so it's crucial to be ready for both warm afternoons and cool mornings.

Clothing:

- **Layering Essentials**: Always dress in layers. Mornings can start off chilly, but by midday, you might be shedding a few layers. A base layer made from moisture-wicking material, followed by a fleece or light sweater, and finally, a waterproof jacket will ensure you stay comfortable no matter the conditions.

- **Waterproof Jacket**: Even in summer, rain is common. A good, lightweight waterproof jacket is essential for sudden showers or hikes that lead you near waterfalls like the **Athabasca Falls** or **Bow Falls**.

- **Hiking Boots**: Make sure your hiking boots are broken in and waterproof. The trails can be rocky, muddy, or even snowy at higher elevations, so sturdy footwear with good ankle support is a must. You'll be tackling famous trails like **Larch Valley**, **Peyto Lake**, and the **Valley of the Five Lakes**, which are stunning but can be uneven

- **Breathable Hiking Pants and Shorts**: Convertible hiking pants are a great option because you can zip off the legs if the day gets warm. Quick-drying,

44

breathable fabrics will keep you comfortable on long hikes.

- **Hat and Sunglasses**: Protect yourself from the intense sun, especially at higher elevations. A wide-brimmed hat provides shade, and polarized sunglasses will help reduce the glare from lakes and glaciers.

- **Bug Spray**: Mosquitoes can be persistent in the summer, especially near water sources and at dusk. Packing a good insect repellent is highly recommended.

Gear:

- **Daypack with Hydration Bladder**: A daypack with space for a hydration system is ideal for keeping your hands free while hiking. You'll want to carry snacks, extra layers, and a first-aid kit on longer hikes.

- **Bear Spray**: Both Banff and Jasper are home to black bears and grizzly bears, and while encounters are rare, it's always better to be prepared. Bear spray is available for rent or purchase at many locations in the parks.

- **Trekking Poles**: Useful for longer hikes or steeper trails, trekking poles can help reduce strain on your knees and improve stability.

- **Portable Charger**: If you're using your phone for maps or photography, a portable battery charger is essential, especially on full-day hikes.

Summer Specific Tips:

- **Hydrate Regularly**: High elevations can make you feel dehydrated more quickly, so pack a reusable water bottle or a hydration pack with at least 2 liters of water.

- **Pack for All Weather**: Even in the summer, temperatures can drop in the evening or at higher elevations, so always bring a warmer layer for when the sun sets.

Winter Packing List (November to March)

Winter in Banff and Jasper turns the parks into a snowy wonderland, perfect for skiing, snowshoeing, and ice walks. However, winter can be harsh, and the right gear is vital to staying safe and warm.

Clothing:

- **Base Layers (Thermal Clothing)**: Start with a good pair of moisture-wicking thermal layers. Merino wool or synthetic materials are best for keeping you warm and dry.

- **Insulating Layers**: On top of your base layer, wear an insulating layer like a fleece or down jacket to trap body heat. Opt for packable down jackets that are lightweight but extremely warm.

- **Waterproof Outer Layer**: A windproof and waterproof outer layer is a must to protect you from the snow and wind. A high-quality ski jacket and snow pants will provide extra warmth and protection against the elements, especially if you're skiing at **Lake Louise Ski Resort** or **Marmot Basin** in Jasper

- **Gloves, Hat, and Neck Gaiter**: Extremities are the first to get cold, so invest in insulated gloves and a warm hat that covers your ears. A neck gaiter or scarf will help protect your face from icy winds.

- **Winter Boots**: Insulated, waterproof boots with good traction are a must for walking on snow and ice. You'll need them for activities like snowshoeing or visiting frozen waterfalls like **Johnston Canyon** in Banff or **Maligne Canyon** in Jasper.

- **Thermal Socks**: Bring several pairs of wool or synthetic thermal socks. Cold feet can ruin your day quickly, especially when out on the trails for hours.

Gear:

- **Snowshoes or Crampons**: If you're planning to do some winter hiking or exploring icy paths like the **Athabasca Glacier**, you'll need snowshoes or crampons to safely navigate the snow and ice.

- **Ski Equipment (or Rental Info)**: If you're skiing or snowboarding, either bring your gear or plan to rent from the numerous rental shops in Banff and Jasper. Most ski resorts, like **Sunshine Village** and **Marmot Basin**, offer rentals, but booking in advance is a good idea during peak winter season.

- **Hand and Foot Warmers**: Disposable or rechargeable hand and foot warmers can make a huge difference when temperatures drop below freezing.

- **Headlamp**: Winter days are short, and if you're out on the trails or driving, a headlamp is essential in case you're caught after dark. Make sure it's fully charged and bright enough to light your path in snowy conditions.

Winter Specific Tips:

- **Layering is Key**: In winter, you'll want to dress in layers that you can adjust throughout the day as you heat up from activity or cool down when stopping for breaks. Start with a moisture-wicking base layer and build up with insulation and waterproof layers.

- **Stay Hydrated**: Even though it's cold, dehydration can happen quickly. Carry a thermos with hot tea or water to stay warm and hydrated on the go.

- **Drive Carefully**: Winter roads can be icy, so make sure your vehicle is equipped with snow tires, or rent a car with snow tires if you're driving to locations like **Maligne Lake** or **Lake Minnewanka.**

Year-Round Essentials

- **Park Pass**: You'll need a park pass for entry into Banff and Jasper National Parks. These can be purchased at park gates or online and should always be displayed on your vehicle's dashboard.

- **Reusable Water Bottle**: No matter the season, staying hydrated is important. Bring a reusable water bottle and refill at stations or streams (after proper filtration).

- **Map and Compass**: Although smartphones are great, they can lose battery or signal. A physical map of the parks and a compass are reliable backups for navigation.

Winter Sports Equipment and Warm Clothing.

When preparing for winter sports and activities in Banff and Jasper, having the right gear and safety essentials is crucial for an enjoyable and safe experience. Here's a breakdown of what you'll need, along with some commonly forgotten items and safety tips for dealing with the unpredictable mountain weather.

Winter Sports Equipment and Warm Clothing:

Clothing for Winter Activities:

- **Thermal Base Layers**: These are non-negotiable. Start with a moisture-wicking layer to keep sweat away from your skin. Merino wool or synthetic materials like polyester work best.

- **Insulating Layers**: Choose a mid-layer like a fleece jacket or a down-filled jacket. These layers trap body heat while allowing moisture to escape, keeping you warm and dry.

- **Waterproof and Windproof Outer Layer**: A good quality, insulated ski jacket and snow pants are essential to protect you from snow, wind, and freezing temperatures. Make sure these layers are breathable to prevent overheating during physical activities.

- **Winter Boots**: Insulated, waterproof boots with good traction are necessary for snowshoeing, ice walks, or even strolling around town in icy conditions. Brands that specialize in winter gear like Sorel or Columbia are popular choices.

- **Gloves, Hat, and Scarf**: Your extremities are particularly vulnerable to cold. Insulated, waterproof gloves, a wool or fleece hat that covers your ears, and a scarf or neck gaiter will protect you from frostbite.

- **Snowshoes or Crampons**: If you plan to explore trails on foot, snowshoes are essential for deep snow. For icy paths, crampons (spikes that attach to your boots) are useful for traction and stability.

- **Ski and Snowboard Gear**: If skiing or snowboarding, bring your own equipment or rent from one of the many shops in the parks. Ensure your gear is well-maintained and that you're familiar with your equipment before hitting the slopes. Helmets are a must for safety.

First Aid, Navigation Tools, and Safety Tips:

- **First Aid Kit**: It's always a good idea to carry a small, well-stocked first aid kit, especially if you plan to venture into more remote areas. Include bandages, antiseptic wipes, pain relievers, blister treatments, and any personal medications.

- **Map and Compass/GPS**: While phone maps are convenient, it's crucial to have a physical map and a compass or GPS as a backup. Batteries drain faster in cold weather, and phone signals can be unreliable in some parts of the parks. Detailed maps of Banff and Jasper are available at visitor centers and can be downloaded before your trip.

- **Headlamp**: In winter, daylight hours are short, and if you're out on the trails in the afternoon, a headlamp can be essential for safe navigation after dark. Make sure it's fully charged or has fresh batteries.

- **Avalanche Safety Gear**: If you plan on doing any backcountry skiing or snowboarding, carry avalanche safety equipment, including a beacon, probe, and shovel, and ensure you know how to use them. Taking an avalanche safety course is highly recommended.

Commonly Forgotten Items (and Must-Haves):

- **Bear Spray**: While bears are less active in winter, they aren't entirely dormant, especially early or late in the season. Carry bear spray and know how to use it, just in case. In summer, bear spray is essential at all times.

- **Mosquito Repellent**: During the summer months, especially near lakes and wetlands, mosquitoes can be a nuisance. Pack a strong insect repellent to avoid bites when hiking near water or in the evening.

- **Sunscreen and Lip Balm**: Even in winter, the sun can be strong, especially when reflected off the snow. Sunscreen is essential to avoid sunburn, and lip balm with SPF will help prevent chapped lips.

- **Hand and Foot Warmers**: These disposable or rechargeable warmers can be lifesavers during cold snaps, especially if you're outdoors for long periods.

- **Water Bottle or Hydration System**: Dehydration can sneak up on you even in cold weather. Carry an insulated water bottle to prevent freezing or use a hydration pack with an insulated hose if you're hiking or skiing.

- **Extra Batteries**: Cold weather drains batteries faster, so pack extras for your headlamp, GPS, or camera.

Preparing for Varying Weather Conditions:

Mountain weather is notoriously unpredictable, and it's common to experience all four seasons in a single day, even in summer. Here's how to prepare:

- **Layering**: In both summer and winter, the key to comfort is layering. By dressing in several thin layers, you can adjust to changing conditions by adding or removing layers as needed.

- **Check the Weather**: Always check the forecast before heading out for the day. Weather conditions can change rapidly in the mountains, and being prepared for sudden shifts is crucial. If you're going on a longer hike or ski trip, ask about the conditions at the local visitor centers.

- **Pack Extra Clothes**: If you're hiking or out for a long day in winter, bring an extra pair of socks and gloves in case your originals get wet. Keeping your feet and hands dry is critical for staying warm.

- **Be Aware of Frostbite and Hypothermia**: Know the signs of frostbite and hypothermia, especially if you're spending long periods outdoors. Frostbite usually affects the fingers, toes, nose, and ears. If you feel numbness or tingling, take a break and warm up inside. Hypothermia can be life-threatening, so always ensure you have a plan to warm up if the temperature drops suddenly.

Chapter 6

Must-See Sights in Banff National Park.

Banff National Park offers a mix of breathtaking landscapes, iconic sights, and hidden gems that reward the adventurous. While top spots like **Lake Louise** and the **Banff Gondola** attract crowds, savvy travelers can plan strategically to avoid the busiest times and explore less-trodden paths for a more serene experience. Here's a comprehensive guide to must-see sights, hidden gems, and practical booking tips to help you make the most of your visit.

1. Lake Louise: A Natural Wonder

Lake Louise is undoubtedly one of Banff's most famous landmarks, and for good reason. Its stunning turquoise waters, surrounded by the towering peaks of the Rocky Mountains, create an unforgettable scene. However, this popularity also means it can be quite crowded, particularly in the summer.

How Best to Explore:

- **Arrive Early**: The best way to experience Lake Louise without the throngs of tourists is to arrive at sunrise. The early morning light casts a soft glow over the lake, and you'll have the place mostly to yourself. The parking lot fills up fast, so aim to arrive by 7 a.m. to secure a spot.
- **Winter Visits**: For a quieter experience, visit Lake Louise in the winter, when the lake freezes over. You can ice skate across its surface or take a horse-drawn sleigh ride along the snowy shores.

Booking Tips:

- **Shuttle Services**: If you miss the early morning window, consider using the Parks Canada shuttle service from Banff or Lake Louise Village to avoid the hassle of parking.
- **Accommodation**: Staying at the **Fairmont Chateau Lake Louise** gives you prime access to the lake before the day crowds arrive. It's a luxurious option, but worth it for the unbeatable views and exclusive early access.

2. Moraine Lake: The Crown Jewel of the Rockies

Moraine Lake, set in the Valley of the Ten Peaks, is often considered even more picturesque than Lake Louise, with its deep blue waters reflecting the towering peaks around it. The lake is another must-see, but it has become increasingly difficult to visit due to its limited parking and overwhelming popularity.

How Best to Explore:

- **Shuttle Only**: As of recent years, Moraine Lake's parking lot has been closed to private vehicles, making shuttle services the only way to visit. Book your shuttle in advance to ensure a spot. Private tours and taxis are also an option for accessing the lake.

- **Sunrise and Sunset Visits**: Like Lake Louise, the best time to visit Moraine Lake is at sunrise or sunset. The light at these times is magical and transforms the lake into an ethereal landscape. The hike to **Consolation Lakes** from Moraine Lake also provides an alternative, less crowded.

Booking Tips:

- **Plan Months in Advance**: Especially during peak season, book your shuttle tickets months ahead of time. Consider going during the shoulder season (May or late September) for a quieter visit.

- **Stay Close By**: Staying in Lake Louise Village allows for easier access to the shuttles.

3. Banff Gondola & Sulphur Mountain: Iconic Views

Riding the **Banff Gondola** up Sulphur Mountain provides some of the best panoramic views of Banff and the Bow Valley. Once at the top, there are walking paths, observation decks, and restaurants to enjoy.

How Best to Explore:

- **Hike Up, Gondola Down**: For a more adventurous experience, hike the Sulphur Mountain Trail (a 5.5-kilometer switchback trail) to the summit and take the gondola back down. This lets you enjoy the mountain's natural beauty while avoiding crowds during the ascent.

- **Visit in Shoulder Season**: While the gondola is open year-round, visiting in the shoulder season (April to May or late September) provides a more tranquil experience. Winter gondola rides offer a unique opportunity to see snow-covered peaks.

Booking Tips:

- **Book in Advance**: During the summer, gondola tickets sell out quickly, so reserve yours well ahead of time. Booking online in advance often gives you a discount.

- **Sunset Package**: For a romantic evening, consider booking the sunset dinner package, where you can enjoy a meal at **Sky Bistro** while watching the sun dip below the mountains.

4. Johnston Canyon: A Waterfall Wonderland

Johnston Canyon is one of the most popular day hikes in Banff, thanks to its relatively easy trail and stunning waterfalls. The catwalks that wind through the canyon provide incredible views of the cascading water.

How Best to Explore:

- **Beat the Crowds**: This is a very busy spot, especially in the middle of the day. The best time to hike here is early morning or late afternoon. If you're visiting in winter, Johnston Canyon transforms into a spectacular ice walk with frozen waterfalls and icy cliffs.

- **Beyond the Upper Falls**: Most visitors turn around after reaching the Upper Falls, but if you continue a bit farther, you'll reach the quieter **Ink Pots**. These scenic mineral pools offer a peaceful retreat and a less crowded destination.

Booking Tips:

- **Guided Ice Walks**: In winter, consider booking a guided ice walk, which includes gear rentals like crampons and expert commentary on the canyon's geology and ice formations.

- **Nearby Accommodation**: Stay at **Castle Mountain Chalets**, located halfway between Banff and Johnston Canyon, for easy access to the canyon while avoiding the crowds in Banff Town.

5. Peyto Lake: A Glacial Gem

Peyto Lake's vibrant blue color and wolf-head shape make it one of the most photogenic lakes in Banff National Park. Located along the Icefields Parkway, it offers a quick but rewarding stop.

How Best to Explore:

- **Visit at Dusk or Dawn**: The Peyto Lake lookout is popular with tour buses, but arriving early in the morning or late in the evening will give you a much more peaceful experience. The soft light during these times is also perfect for photography.

- **Extend Your Hike**: While the main lookout is just a short walk from the parking lot, extending your hike onto the **Bow Summit** trail will reward you with fewer people and stunning panoramic views

Booking Tips:

- **Avoid Midday Tours**: Many visitors arrive via tour buses between 10 a.m. and 3 p.m., so plan your visit outside of these hours for a quieter experience.

- **Combine with Icefields Parkway**: Plan your visit to Peyto Lake as part of a larger Icefields Parkway day trip, where you can explore other lesser-known stops like **Mistaya Canyon** or **Bow Lake**.

Hidden Gems and Less Crowded Areas

Boom Lake

While the iconic spots draw large crowds, **Boom Lake** offers a quieter, more serene experience. Located west of Banff, the trail to Boom Lake is a moderate 5.1-kilometer hike that leads to a picturesque alpine lake surrounded by towering cliffs. It's a great spot for a peaceful picnic or just soaking in the scenery without the crowds.

- **Tip**: This trail is less popular, even during peak season, so it's perfect for those looking for a quieter hike.

Marble Canyon

Located on the way to Kootenay National Park, **Marble Canyon** is often overlooked by visitors who flock to Johnston Canyon. However, it offers a similarly stunning walk through a deep limestone gorge with waterfalls and bridges spanning the canyon. This is a great alternative if you want a similar experience with fewer people.

- **Tip**: Combine a visit to Marble Canyon with the **Paint Pots** nearby for a full day of exploring lesser-known spots in the park.

Parker Ridge Trail

For jaw-dropping views without the heavy crowds, the **Parker Ridge Trail** off the Icefields Parkway offers an exceptional experience. It's a short but steep 5-kilometer round trip hike that leads to views of the Saskatchewan Glacier, a massive icefield feeding the Columbia Icefield.

- **Tip**: While this trail is well-known among locals and avid hikers, it remains relatively uncrowded compared to more accessible trails like Lake Louise. It's also best visited in late summer when the snow has melted.

Quick Tips for Avoiding Crowds at Iconic Spots:

Visit Early or Late: As with most national parks, the best way to avoid crowds is to visit early in the morning (before 8 a.m.) or late in the afternoon (after 4 p.m.). These hours provide not only quieter experiences but also better lighting for photography.

Shoulder Season Travel: Late May or early September are ideal times to visit Banff, as the weather is still pleasant, but the summer rush has subsided.

Use Shuttles and Public Transport: Parking at popular spots like Lake Louise and Moraine Lake can be a hassle. Use the shuttle services to avoid wasting time hunting for a spot, and plan your stops accordingly.

Midweek Visits: If your schedule allows, aim to visit popular spots midweek (Tuesday-Thursday) when visitor numbers are lower than on weekends.

Chapter 7

Top Attractions in Jasper National Park

Jasper National Park, known for its rugged beauty and serene landscapes, offers some of the most breathtaking natural wonders in the Canadian Rockies. From thundering waterfalls to tranquil lakes surrounded by towering peaks, here are the top attractions you should explore:

1. Athabasca Falls

Athabasca Falls is one of Jasper's most powerful and mesmerizing waterfalls. Despite not being the tallest, its force and volume make it an unforgettable sight. The waterfall, fed by the Athabasca River, plunges through a narrow gorge, creating dramatic cascades and swirling pools below.

- **What Makes it Special**: The sheer power of the water and the canyon it has carved over thousands of years. Visitors can safely explore the viewing platforms and trails that wrap around the falls, offering different perspectives of the rushing water and the mist that rises from the falls.

- **Best Time to Visit**: Early morning or late evening during the summer months offers fewer crowds and beautiful soft light. In winter, the frozen falls become an ice-covered spectacle, perfect for photography.

Travel Tip: Athabasca Falls is easily accessible by car, with plenty of parking and well-maintained paths. It's a short walk from the parking area to the falls, making it ideal for visitors of all ages.

2. Maligne Lake

Maligne Lake, the second-largest glacial-fed lake in the world, is often described as the crown jewel of Jasper National Park. Its striking blue waters, framed by the snow-capped Rockies, make it one of the most scenic spots in the park. The lake is also famous for **Spirit Island**, a small, iconic island that's often featured in photographs of Jasper.

- **What Makes it Special**: Maligne Lake's color and clarity are unmatched. The surrounding peaks create a dramatic backdrop, and Spirit Island is a must-see, accessible only by boat tour. The boat cruises take you to this tranquil spot, where you can disembark briefly for photos and a walk around the area.

- **Best Time to Visit**: The summer months are the best for visiting, as the lake is fully thawed and vibrant. Early morning and late afternoon are great for avoiding crowds.

Travel Tip: Consider taking a guided Maligne Lake Cruise to Spirit Island. It's the best way to experience the lake's beauty up close. If you prefer staying on land, hiking the Mary Schäffer Loop offers panoramic views of the lake without the need for a boat tour.

3. Columbia Icefield and Athabasca Glacier

The **Columbia Icefield**, one of the largest icefields in North America, is home to the Athabasca Glacier. This massive ice sheet is both a historical wonder and a striking example of how glaciers have shaped the landscape over millennia.

- **What Makes it Special**: Standing on the glacier itself is a once-in-a-lifetime experience. Specially designed Ice Explorer vehicles take visitors right onto the glacier, where you can walk on the ancient ice and drink glacial water. The **Columbia Icefield Skywalk**, a glass-floored observation platform, offers dizzying views of the Sunwapta Valley below.
- **Best Time to Visit**: The summer months (May through October) provide the best conditions for visiting the glacier and experiencing the Ice Explorer tour.

Travel Tip: Book your glacier tour in advance, as spots fill up quickly during peak season. The nearby Glacier Discovery Centre offers informative exhibits and dining options with spectacular glacier views.

4. Mount Edith Cavell and Angel Glacier

Mount Edith Cavell, one of the most prominent peaks in Jasper, offers some of the park's most striking landscapes. The **Angel Glacier**, located on the mountain's north face, is named for its wing-like appearance and can be viewed from several hiking trails.

- **What Makes it Special**: Mount Edith Cavell combines towering rocky slopes with lush valleys below. Angel Glacier's massive ice formations are a rare sight and make for a fantastic backdrop for photos. Hiking in this area provides close-up views of glacial moraines, icebergs floating in meltwater pools, and abundant wildflowers in the summer.

- **Best Time to Visit**: Late spring to early fall is the best time for hiking around Mount Edith Cavell, though the glacier is stunning year-round. Be aware that the access road is closed in winter due to avalanche risk.

Travel Tip: The Path of the Glacier Trail is a short but rewarding hike that leads you to the base of the glacier. Early in the morning, before the crowds arrive, is the perfect time to enjoy the tranquil beauty of the glacier without interruption

5. Maligne Canyon

Maligne Canyon is one of the deepest canyons in the Canadian Rockies, and it offers an exciting experience as you walk along its rim and peer down into the depths. Water from Maligne Lake flows through the canyon, carving it deeper with each passing year.

- **What Makes it Special**: The intricate limestone formations and the powerful flow of water create spectacular scenes at every turn. In winter, the canyon becomes even more magical as the waterfalls freeze into towering icicles, and you can walk along the frozen canyon floor with a guided ice walk tour.

- **Best Time to Visit**: The canyon is accessible year-round, but summer and fall are ideal for hiking along the rim. In winter, the frozen waterfalls and ice-covered canyon floor make for an incredible adventure on an ice walk.

Travel Tip: If you're visiting in winter, a guided ice walk tour is a must for a safe and exhilarating way to explore the canyon from below

6. Pyramid Lake and Pyramid Island

For those seeking a more peaceful and serene setting, **Pyramid Lake** is a gem in Jasper National Park. The lake, with **Pyramid Mountain** as a stunning backdrop, offers calm waters perfect for canoeing, fishing, or simply enjoying the view.

- **What Makes it Special**: Pyramid Lake's proximity to Jasper townsite makes it an easy spot to visit for a half-day or afternoon outing. A short bridge leads you to **Pyramid Island**, where you can enjoy a quiet walk, picnic, or simply relax with the breathtaking mountain views.

- **Best Time to Visit**: Summer offers the best conditions for water activities, while fall provides gorgeous colors as the leaves turn. Pyramid Lake is also stunning in winter, when you can skate on its frozen surface.

Travel Tip: Rent a canoe or kayak from the nearby boathouse for a relaxing paddle around the lake. It's also a great spot for photography at sunrise or sunset, when the light reflects off the still waters.

Hidden Gems in Jasper National Park: Serene, Less-Crowded Spots

1. Sunwapta Falls

Though smaller than Athabasca Falls, **Sunwapta Falls** offers a more intimate and equally beautiful experience. The falls are divided into upper and lower sections, with powerful water plunging over limestone cliffs.

- **Tip**: Visit early in the morning or late in the evening for a quieter experience. The short trail to the lower falls is less frequented and offers a peaceful walk through the forest.

2. Medicine Lake

Medicine Lake is a unique geological phenomenon, as it drains completely in the fall and reappears in spring due to underground sinkholes. This disappearing lake is located along the road to Maligne Lake and offers a peaceful place for a picnic or short hike.

- **Tip**: Stop here on your way to Maligne Lake for a quieter experience with equally stunning views. Medicine Lake is often overlooked by those heading straight to Maligne.

3. Geraldine Lakes

The **Geraldine Lakes** are a series of alpine lakes accessible by a challenging but rewarding hike. The trail is rugged and steep, but the views of the pristine lakes and surrounding peaks are worth the effort.

- **Tip**: This trail is perfect for experienced hikers looking for a more secluded adventure. You'll likely have the trail mostly to yourself, especially in the shoulder seasons.

Wildlife Viewing, Canoeing, & Horseback Riding.

Jasper National Park is one of the premier wildlife viewing locations in North America, where visitors can encounter a wide array of animals in their natural habitat. The vast, undisturbed wilderness provides opportunities to see iconic Canadian species like grizzly bears, elk, wolves, and bighorn sheep. Beyond wildlife viewing, Jasper also offers adventurous activities like canoeing, horseback riding, and guided wilderness tours. Here's a detailed guide to help you make the most of your wildlife encounters and adventure experiences in Jasper National Park.

Best Wildlife Viewing Locations and What You Might See

Jasper is teeming with wildlife, thanks to its varied ecosystems of forests, lakes, rivers, and alpine meadows. Here are some of the best places to spot wildlife, along with the animals you're most likely to encounter:

1. Maligne Lake and Maligne Valley

The Maligne Valley, stretching from Medicine Lake to Maligne Lake, is one of the best places in Jasper to spot wildlife. The valley is known for frequent sightings of **moose**, which are often seen wading through shallow waters near Maligne Lake.

- **What to See**: Keep an eye out for **grizzly bears**, **black bears**, **elk**, **deer**, and **mountain goats** along this route. The area around Medicine Lake, in particular, is great for bear sightings, especially during the late spring and early summer when the animals are foraging for food.

- **Best Times**: Early mornings and evenings offer the best chances for spotting wildlife, as animals are most active during these cooler parts of the day.

- **Pro Tip**: Take a cruise on Maligne Lake for a quieter way to spot wildlife along the shoreline. The cruise to **Spirit Island** provides incredible views of the lake and is a fantastic opportunity to see animals that gather near the water.

2. Pyramid Lake and Pyramid Bench

Located just minutes from Jasper townsite, **Pyramid Lake** and the surrounding **Pyramid Bench** are fantastic places for wildlife enthusiasts. The trails around this area offer quiet, scenic views of the lake and its surroundings, making it a great spot for **elk, deer**, and **beavers**. In winter, you might even see wolves hunting in the distance or their tracks along the snowy trails.

- **What to See**: Elk are common in the area, especially in fall during the rutting season when you might hear the haunting calls of male elk competing for mates. The **Pyramid Lake** area is also home to many small mammals like **foxes**, **porcupines**, and even the elusive **lynx**.

- **Pro Tip**: The early morning is the best time to see animals along the shores of Pyramid Lake. You can also take a canoe or kayak out on the water for a peaceful wildlife viewing experience from a unique vantage point.

3. Jasper's Icefields Parkway

The **Icefields Parkway** is not only one of the most scenic drives in the world but also a prime location for wildlife sightings. The road connects Jasper with Banff, running through a rich landscape filled with wildlife.

- **What to See**: Along this route, you'll often spot **bighorn sheep**, **mountain goats**, **caribou**, and **grizzly bears**. The cliffs near **Sunwapta Falls** and the **Athabasca Glacier** are known for sightings of bighorn sheep and mountain goats. Bears are commonly seen crossing the road or foraging along the edges of the forest.

- **Best Times**: Wildlife is most active along the parkway early in the morning and late in the evening, and these quieter hours also mean fewer vehicles on the road.

- **Pro Tip**: Drive slowly and be prepared to pull over at wildlife crossings, but remember to keep a safe distance and never feed or approach animals. If you're a photographer, bring a zoom lens to capture shots from afar.

4. Jasper Townsite and Surrounding Area

Even within and around the town of Jasper itself, you can often see **elk** strolling down the streets or foraging in the open grassy areas. During the fall rutting season, elk can be seen sparring with their antlers and calling loudly. The area surrounding **Lake Annette** and **Lake Edith** near the town are other good spots for spotting **elk** and **deer**.

- **Pro Tip**: Jasper's townsite offers plenty of wildlife sightings right from your hotel window or while walking through town. However, remember to give animals their space, especially during mating seasons.

Adventurous Activities: Canoeing, Horseback Riding.

Beyond wildlife viewing, Jasper National Park is a paradise for adventure lovers. There are plenty of activities to get your adrenaline pumping or to help you connect with nature in a more active way.

1. Canoeing and Kayaking

Canoeing and kayaking are popular activities in Jasper, particularly on the calm, clear waters of **Maligne Lake, Pyramid Lake**, and **Lac Beauvert**.

- **Maligne Lake**: Renting a canoe at Maligne Lake allows you to paddle across its pristine waters and soak in the dramatic scenery. You might also spot wildlife along the shoreline as you quietly glide through the water.

- **Pyramid Lake**: Pyramid Lake offers an equally peaceful paddling experience, with incredible views of Pyramid Mountain. Canoes, kayaks, and paddleboards can be rented at the lake's boathouse.

- **Booking Tip**: Canoe and kayak rentals are available at **Maligne Lake Boathouse** and **Pyramid Lake Resort**. It's a good idea to book in advance during peak season, especially on weekends. Many lodges and resorts in the area, like the **Fairmont Jasper Park Lodge,** also offer watercraft rentals for guests

2. Horseback Riding

Exploring Jasper on horseback offers a unique and memorable way to experience the rugged beauty of the park. Several companies provide guided horseback rides along scenic trails, offering views of mountain landscapes, forests, and even some secluded wildlife viewing opportunities.

- **Jasper Riding Stables**: Located near the Jasper townsite, **Jasper Riding Stables** offers trail rides that range from one-hour excursions to full-day adventures. Riders of all experience levels are welcome, and the stables offer stunning routes that lead through the foothills of the Rockies and along scenic rivers.

- **Outpost Riding Stables**: This stable, located near Pyramid Lake, provides another excellent option for horseback riding in Jasper. The tours take you along winding trails, through alpine meadows, and up to beautiful viewpoints.

- **Booking Tip**: Reservations are highly recommended, especially during the summer months. It's best to book a few weeks in advance if you're planning to visit during July or August. Group rides can be arranged, and some stables offer private, customized tours for a more personalized experience.

3. Whitewater Rafting

For the more adventurous traveler, whitewater rafting on the **Athabasca River** or the **Sunwapta River** is a thrilling way to see the park from a different perspective. The rivers offer a range of rapids, from gentle Class II to more challenging Class III rapids.

- **Athabasca River**: This river is perfect for beginners and families. The rafting trips here offer gentle rapids and plenty of opportunities to take in the views of the surrounding mountains and valleys. Wildlife sightings from the river, such as eagles, elk, and even bears, are not uncommon.

- **Sunwapta River**: For those seeking more excitement, the Sunwapta River's Class III rapids provide an exhilarating ride. This fast-moving river cuts through a scenic canyon, offering both a thrilling and picturesque adventure.

- **Booking Tip**: Whitewater rafting tours are available from several companies, including **Jasper Raft Tours** and **Maligne Rafting Adventures**. It's best to book ahead, especially for the more popular tours during peak season. Many tours provide all necessary gear, including wetsuits and helmets.

4. Rock Climbing and Mountaineering

For those seeking a vertical challenge, Jasper offers excellent opportunities for rock climbing and mountaineering. With routes ranging from beginner to expert, there's something for climbers of all skill levels.

- **Famous Climbing Spots**: **Old Fort Point**, just a short drive from Jasper townsite, is one of the most popular climbing areas. For experienced mountaineers, summiting **Mount Edith Cavell** offers an extraordinary adventure with unbeatable views at the top.

- **Guided Tours**: Several companies in Jasper offer guided climbing tours and mountaineering experiences for those new to the sport. You can learn basic techniques or embark on more challenging climbs with expert guides.

- **Booking Tip**: It's essential to book guided climbs in advance, especially for technical routes like Mount Edith Cavell. Companies like **Jasper Rock & Ice** provide guided tours, equipment rentals, and expert instruction.

Final Thoughts

Jasper National Park offers both incredible wildlife viewing and countless opportunities for adventure. Whether you're canoeing across a serene lake, riding horseback through alpine meadows, or seeking out Jasper's most elusive animals, this vast park promises an unforgettable experience. Planning ahead and booking activities early, especially in peak season, ensures you can make the most of your time in this breathtaking wilderness.

Chapter 8

Outdoor Adventures: Hiking, Biking.

Jasper and Banff National Parks offer an extensive range of hiking trails that cater to all skill levels. Whether you're a beginner looking for a gentle hike or an advanced hiker seeking a multi-day backcountry adventure, these parks have something for everyone. Here's a guide to the best hiking trails in both parks, categorized by difficulty level.

Best Hiking Trails for Beginners

1. Lake Annette and Lake Edith Loop (Jasper)

- **Difficulty**: Easy
- **Distance**: 2.4 kilometers round trip

- **Elevation Gain**: Minimal
- **Description**: This loop around Lake Annette and Lake Edith is perfect for those looking for a gentle stroll with scenic views. The trail is flat, well-maintained, and offers picturesque views of the lakes and surrounding mountains. It's a family-friendly hike, ideal for a relaxed day out in nature.

2. Bow River Loop (Banff)

- **Difficulty**: Easy
- **Distance**: 6 kilometers round trip
- **Elevation Gain**: Minimal
- **Description**: This flat, easy trail follows the Bow River and offers great views of the Banff townsite and surrounding mountains. It's a peaceful, family-friendly trail that allows you to enjoy the river and take in some of Banff's best sights without much effort.

3. Pyramid Lake Loop (Jasper)

- **Difficulty**: Easy
- **Distance**: 5 kilometers round trip
- **Elevation Gain**: 100 meters
- **Description**: This serene loop around Pyramid Lake is another great option for beginners. The trail offers beautiful views of Pyramid Mountain, especially at sunrise or sunset, and provides opportunities for

spotting wildlife. The gentle elevation gain makes it accessible to most hikers.

Best Hiking Trails for Intermediates.

1. Valley of the Five Lakes (Jasper)

- **Difficulty**: Moderate
- **Distance**: 4.5 kilometers round trip
- **Elevation Gain**: 66 meters
- **Description**: This popular hike takes you through forested areas and along five beautiful emerald-green lakes. Each lake has a unique shade of blue or green, and there are plenty of opportunities for scenic photos. While the trail isn't overly challenging, it does have some rolling hills, making it perfect for intermediate hikers.

2. Larch Valley/Sentinel Pass (Banff)

- **Difficulty**: Moderate
- **Distance**: 11.6 kilometers round trip
- **Elevation Gain**: 723 meters
- **Description**: Starting at Moraine Lake, this trail takes you up to the stunning Larch Valley, which is famous for its golden larches in the fall. If you're up for a bit more of a challenge, continue on to Sentinel Pass, where you'll be rewarded with expansive views of the Ten Peaks. The steep switchbacks make this

hike more suited to those with some hiking experience.

3. Sulphur Skyline (Jasper)

- **Difficulty**: Moderate
- **Distance**: 8 kilometers round trip
- **Elevation Gain**: 700 meters
- **Description**: This trail rewards hikers with some of the best panoramic views in Jasper. Starting from the **Miette Hot Springs**, the trail climbs steadily through forested areas before emerging onto the exposed summit ridge, offering incredible views of the surrounding mountains and valleys. After the hike, you can relax in the hot springs, making it a perfect day trip.

Best Hiking Trails for Advanced Hikers

1. The Skyline Trail (Jasper)

- **Difficulty**: Advanced
- **Distance**: 44 kilometers one way
- **Elevation Gain**: 1,287 meters
- **Description**: One of Jasper's premier backcountry trails, the Skyline Trail offers an unforgettable experience for seasoned hikers. The trail takes you across high alpine meadows and ridgelines, providing uninterrupted views of the rugged

mountains. Most of the trail is above the tree line, offering a dramatic and isolated wilderness experience. It's best done as a multi-day hike, with campsites available along the route.

2. Mount Temple (Banff)

- **Difficulty**: Advanced
- **Distance**: 16 kilometers round trip
- **Elevation Gain**: 1,691 meters
- **Description**: Mount Temple is a challenging and iconic hike in Banff National Park, offering experienced hikers a chance to summit one of the tallest peaks in the area. The trail begins at **Moraine Lake** and climbs steeply through forests, alpine meadows, and rocky slopes. The views from the summit are nothing short of spectacular, but the ascent requires good physical fitness and hiking experience. Be prepared for snow, even in the summer.

3. Cory Pass (Banff)

- **Difficulty**: Advanced
- **Distance**: 13 kilometers round trip
- **Elevation Gain**: 915 meters
- **Description**: The **Cory Pass** hike offers steep climbs and dramatic views of Mount Louis and the surrounding valleys. This trail is a strenuous day

hike, but the panoramic views from the pass make the effort worthwhile. The steep ascent and rocky terrain require good stamina and experience, and the loop through Edith Pass adds some variation to the hike.

Additional Outdoor Adventures in Banff and Jasper

Beyond hiking, both Jasper and Banff offer a wide range of outdoor activities for those who want to explore the parks in different ways:

Biking

- **Banff Legacy Trail (Banff)**: This scenic 26-kilometer trail is perfect for cyclists of all abilities and runs from Banff to Canmore. It's a paved trail with beautiful mountain views and is ideal for those wanting a longer, but relatively easy, bike ride.
- **Overlander Trail (Jasper)**: A moderately challenging trail, the Overlander offers both single-track biking and incredible views of the Athabasca River.

Climbing

- **Old Fort Point (Jasper)**: Popular for rock climbing and scrambling, this area offers routes suitable for intermediate and advanced climbers looking for a vertical adventure.
- **Cascade Mountain (Banff)**: For experienced climbers, **Cascade Mountain** offers challenging routes with incredible rewards. The summit views span across Banff and its surrounding valleys.

Tips for Hiking and Outdoor Adventures in Banff and Jasper

- **Safety First**: Always check the weather before heading out, especially on high-altitude trails where conditions can change rapidly. Bring bear spray, as both parks are home to black and grizzly bears.

- **Gear Up**: Even for moderate hikes, sturdy hiking boots and layered clothing are essential. Higher elevation hikes may require additional gear like trekking poles and gloves.

- **Permits and Reservations**: For backcountry trails like the Skyline Trail, you'll need to reserve campsites ahead of time. In Banff, some of the busier trails, such as those around Moraine Lake, may require shuttle reservations.

These parks offer a wide variety of trails, allowing you to tailor your adventure to your fitness level and interests. Whether you're seeking a peaceful lakeside stroll or an epic backcountry trek, Banff and Jasper provide some of the best hiking opportunities in the world.

Cycling Routes, Scenic Walks, and Family-Friendly Paths.

Banff and Jasper National Parks offer some of the best biking experiences in the Canadian Rockies. With diverse trails ranging from paved routes for leisurely cyclists to technical mountain biking trails for thrill-seekers, there's a route for every cyclist. In addition to biking, these parks are havens for adventure lovers, offering activities like kayaking, rafting, and rock climbing. Here's a detailed guide to the best biking routes and other adventurous activities in Banff and Jasper.

Top Biking Trails for Scenic Cycling in Banff and Jasper

1. Banff Legacy Trail (Banff)

- **Difficulty**: Easy to Moderate
- **Distance**: 26 kilometers one way
- **Description**: The **Banff Legacy Trail** is one of the most accessible and scenic cycling routes in Banff. The paved pathway runs from the town of Banff to the town of Canmore, offering stunning views of the Bow River, Cascade Mountain, and Rundle Mountain. This trail is perfect for those looking for a leisurely bike ride through the heart of the Rockies.

What to Expect: Along the way, you'll find plenty of rest stops, picnic areas, and scenic viewpoints. It's an ideal trail for families, as it is relatively flat and well-maintained. In the summer, the trail can get busy, so starting early in the morning is recommended for a more peaceful ride.

Best Time to Ride: The trail is open from May to October, but the best time to ride is during the late spring or early fall, when the weather is cooler and the scenery is especially vibrant.

2. Pyramid Lake Road (Jasper)

- **Difficulty**: Moderate
- **Distance**: 12 kilometers round trip
- **Description**: Pyramid Lake Road offers a scenic and moderately challenging ride just minutes from Jasper townsite. The route takes you along a paved road through the forest, offering views of Pyramid Lake and Pyramid Mountain. While it is a road ride, the light traffic and stunning scenery make it feel like a peaceful retreat into nature.

What to Expect: The road climbs steadily for the first half of the ride before leveling out near Pyramid Lake, where you can take a break and enjoy the view or continue onto Pyramid Island for a short walk. This ride is ideal for intermediate cyclists looking for a quiet, scenic escape close to town.

3. Overlander Trail (Jasper)

- **Difficulty**: Moderate to Difficult
- **Distance**: 15 kilometers one way
- **Description**: The **Overlander Trail** offers a mix of single-track biking and stunning views of the Athabasca River and surrounding mountains. It's a challenging route with sections of steep climbs,

rocky terrain, and technical descents, making it more suitable for experienced mountain bikers.

What to Expect: The trail starts near **Jasper House** and winds through forested areas, crossing several ridges that offer panoramic views of the river. Along the way, you'll experience a variety of terrain, including gravel, roots, and rocks. Wildlife sightings are common, so keep your eyes open for elk or deer grazing nearby.

Best Time to Ride: Late spring to early fall is the best time for this trail, as snow can linger in the higher elevations until mid-June.

4. Tunnel Mountain Loop (Banff)

- **Difficulty**: Moderate
- **Distance**: 10 kilometers round trip
- **Description**: The **Tunnel Mountain Loop** offers a great mix of road and off-road biking through one of Banff's most scenic areas. Starting near Banff townsite, this loop takes you along **Tunnel Mountain Road**, passing through forests and meadows with beautiful views of **Cascade Mountain** and the Bow Valley.

What to Expect: The loop is fairly gentle with some gradual climbs, making it a good option for intermediate cyclists. Along the way, you can stop at **Tunnel Mountain Campground** or take a detour to the **Banff Centre** for the Arts. This route is a great option for cyclists looking for a moderate ride with stunning views close to town.

Other Adventurous Activities in Banff and Jasper

Beyond biking, Banff and Jasper National Parks are known for a wide range of adventurous activities that allow visitors to explore the rugged landscapes and pristine waters in thrilling ways.

1. Kayaking and Canoeing

Both Banff and Jasper are home to crystal-clear lakes and rivers that provide perfect conditions for paddling. Whether you're looking for a peaceful day on the water or an adrenaline-pumping adventure, there are options for everyone.

- **Maligne Lake (Jasper)**: **Maligne Lake** is a top destination for canoeing and kayaking. The lake's calm waters are surrounded by towering peaks, and the most famous feature is **Spirit Island**, a small, iconic island in the middle of the lake. Kayak and canoe rentals are available at the **Maligne Lake Boathouse**. If you're up for a challenge, paddling to Spirit Island offers a rewarding experience.

- **Lake Minnewanka (Banff)**: **Lake Minnewanka** is Banff's largest lake and a prime spot for kayaking and canoeing. Its length and depth make it ideal for those looking to explore its many bays and inlets. You can rent kayaks or canoes at the lake or bring your own. The lake's stunning views of the surrounding mountains and crystal-clear waters make it a favorite for paddlers(

2. Whitewater Rafting

For thrill-seekers, whitewater rafting is one of the most popular adventure activities in both parks. The rivers in Banff and Jasper offer a mix of calm sections and rapids ranging from Class II to Class IV, providing excitement for both beginners and experienced rafters.

- **Athabasca River (Jasper)**: The **Athabasca River** offers more gentle rapids, perfect for beginners or families. It's a great way to see wildlife along the riverbanks and experience the park from a different perspective. Several companies, including **Jasper Raft Tours**, offer guided trips down the Athabasca.

- **Kicking Horse River (Banff)**: For a more intense experience, head to the **Kicking Horse River** in Banff, where you'll tackle Class III and IV rapids. This river is perfect for adrenaline junkies looking for fast-paced action. There are several rafting companies that provide all the gear you need, including helmets and wetsuits.

3. Rock Climbing and Mountaineering

The dramatic peaks and craggy cliffs of Banff and Jasper are ideal for rock climbing and mountaineering. Both parks offer routes for climbers of all experience levels, from beginner-friendly climbs to advanced mountaineering.

- **Old Fort Point (Jasper)**: A popular spot for both bouldering and rock climbing, **Old Fort Point** offers several routes for climbers, with some easy scrambles and more technical climbs. It's a great location for beginners and intermediate climbers looking to practice their skills while enjoying stunning views of the Athabasca River and surrounding mountains.

- **Cascade Mountain (Banff)**: For advanced climbers, **Cascade Mountain** provides a challenging but rewarding climb. The summit offers sweeping views of Banff and the Bow Valley. This route is not for the faint of heart and requires good physical fitness, technical climbing skills, and experience with alpine conditions.

4. Horseback Riding

Horseback riding is a quintessential way to experience the Canadian Rockies, especially for those who want to cover more ground while exploring the park's backcountry.

- **Jasper Riding Stables (Jasper)**: **Jasper Riding Stables** offers trail rides that take you through meadows, forests, and foothills, giving you a chance to experience Jasper's wildlife and landscapes in a more traditional way. You can book anything from a one-hour ride to full-day excursions.

- **Banff Trail Riders (Banff)**: In Banff, the **Banff Trail Riders** offer horseback tours through the Bow Valley and along the Bow River. Their trips range from short rides to multi-day backcountry expeditions, complete with overnight stays at wilderness campsites.

Final Tips for Booking Adventures

Book in Advance: Whether you're planning to rent a bike, kayak, or book a rafting or horseback riding tour, it's essential to make reservations ahead of time, especially during the busy summer months. Many adventure companies offer online booking, making it easy to secure your spot.

Check the Weather: Conditions in the Canadian Rockies can change rapidly, so always check the weather before heading out on any adventure. Dress in layers and bring gear for varying conditions, especially if you're planning an all-day activity.

Bring the Right Gear: For biking, kayaking, or hiking, having the right gear can make all the difference. Make sure to wear appropriate footwear, pack a hat and sunscreen, and carry plenty of water. For climbing and mountaineering, ensure you have the necessary equipment and knowledge of the routes.

Chapter 9

Wildlife and Nature: Flora and Fauna.

Banff and Jasper National Parks are rich in biodiversity, offering a wide range of flora and fauna that thrive in the varied ecosystems of the Canadian Rockies. From dense forests and alpine meadows to glacier-fed rivers and lakes, the parks are home to some of North America's most iconic wildlife and plant species. Here's an in-depth look at the animals and plants you can expect to encounter in both parks, as well as the best locations to spot them.

Wildlife in Banff and Jasper

1. Grizzly Bears and Black Bears

Both **grizzly bears** and **black bears** roam the wilderness of Banff and Jasper, though they inhabit different areas. Grizzlies are larger and more aggressive, often found in the higher elevations, while black bears prefer the lower forests and valleys.

- **Best Spots for Bear Watching**:
    - In **Banff**, the best places to see grizzly bears are along the **Bow Valley Parkway** and near **Lake Louise**, especially in the spring and early summer when bears come down to forage.
    - In **Jasper**, try the **Maligne Valley** or along the **Icefields Parkway**. Bears are more commonly seen in the early morning or late evening when they are most active
- **Pro Tip**: Always keep a safe distance (at least 100 meters) and carry bear spray if you're hiking or camping in bear country.

2. Elk

Elk are abundant in both Banff and Jasper and are often seen grazing in meadows, valleys, or even near the towns. They are especially visible in the fall during the rutting season when males gather in large herds and bugle to attract mates.

- **Best Spots for Elk Viewing**:
    - In **Banff**, check out **Bow Valley Parkway** and **Tunnel Mountain**.

- In **Jasper**, they can be frequently spotted around **Pyramid Lake**, **Maligne Lake**, and the townsite itself. Elk tend to wander through town in the early mornings and evenings

3. Bighorn Sheep and Mountain Goats

Bighorn sheep and mountain goats are often spotted on steep, rocky cliffs where they can navigate the terrain with ease. Bighorn sheep are famous for their curled horns, while mountain goats are recognized by their shaggy white coats.

- **Best Spots for Viewing**:
  - **Bighorn Sheep**: Try the **Icefields Parkway** in both parks, especially around **Lake Minnewanka** in Banff and **Athabasca Falls** in Jasper. The cliffs surrounding the highways make excellent habitats for these agile animals.
  - **Mountain Goats**: Look for them along the **Icefields Parkway**, especially around steep cliffs near **Sunwapta Falls** in Jasper and **Bow Lake** in Banff.

4. Wolves and Coyotes

Wolves are elusive, but they do roam the forests of Banff and Jasper. **Coyotes** are more commonly seen, often wandering near highways or open areas in search of food.

- **Best Spots for Spotting**:
  - **Wolves**: You're more likely to hear wolves howling at night, but sightings are rare. For the best chance, head to **Maligne Lake Road**

in Jasper or the **Bow Valley Parkway** in Banff.
- o **Coyotes**: Coyotes are more often seen around **Lake Minnewanka** in Banff or **Pyramid Lake** in Jasper.

5. Moose

Moose, the largest members of the deer family, can be seen in marshy, wetland areas, often feeding on aquatic vegetation.

- **Best Spots for Moose Viewing**:
  - o **Maligne Lake Road** in Jasper is a prime location for moose, particularly near **Medicine Lake** and **Maligne Lake**.
  - o In Banff, moose are less common, but you may spot them near **Vermilion Lakes** or in the backcountry.

6. Caribou

Caribou, another rare but magnificent species, can sometimes be seen in Jasper's high alpine areas. Unlike their larger cousins, the elk, caribou are more elusive and thrive in the park's remote, undisturbed regions.

- **Best Spot for Caribou**: **Tonquin Valley** in Jasper is one of the few areas where these animals might be seen during certain seasons.

Birdwatching

Both Banff and Jasper are havens for bird enthusiasts, home to over 250 species of birds.

Common Birds to Spot:

- **Bald Eagles** and **Golden Eagles** can be seen soaring over lakes and rivers.

- **Ospreys** are often spotted near **Lake Minnewanka** and **Pyramid Lake**, especially during the summer months when they're hunting for fish.

- **Clark's Nutcracker**, **Gray Jays**, and **Black-billed Magpies** are common sightings along hiking trails and campgrounds.

Flora of Banff and Jasper

The parks are also rich in plant life, with distinct vegetation at different elevations and ecosystems.

1. Montane Forests

These lowland forests are found in the valleys and foothills of Banff and Jasper, where temperatures are milder. They are dominated by species like **Douglas fir**, **aspen**, and **lodgepole pine**.

- **Best Spots for Montane Flora**: The **Bow Valley** in Banff and the **Maligne Valley** in Jasper are great places to see these forests. In spring, the forest floors are covered in wildflowers like **wood lilies** and **columbines**.

2. Subalpine Forests

As you climb higher in elevation, the montane forests give way to **subalpine forests**. These forests are dominated by

Engelmann spruce and **subalpine fir**, with an undergrowth of **blueberries** and **bearberries**.

- **Best Spots for Subalpine Flora**: The areas around **Lake Louise** in Banff and **Marmot Basin** in Jasper showcase these forests well. In late summer, the subalpine meadows explode with colorful wildflowers like **Indian paintbrush**, **fireweed**, and **purple aster**.

3. Alpine Tundra

Above the tree line, the hardy plants of the alpine tundra survive in the harsh, windswept conditions. Low-lying plants like **moss campion**, **mountain avens**, and **alpine forget-me-nots** grow close to the ground, clinging to life on the rocky slopes.

- **Best Spots for Alpine Flora**: Hike up to **Sulphur Mountain** in Banff or take the **Whistlers Mountain Tram** in Jasper to explore the unique flora of the alpine zone.

Best Practices for Wildlife and Flora Viewing

- **Keep a Safe Distance**: For your safety and the animals' well-being, always keep at least 30 meters away from elk and deer, and 100 meters away from bears and wolves.
- **Respect Nature**: Avoid picking wildflowers or disturbing wildlife. Stay on marked trails to protect sensitive plant life.
- **Binoculars and Cameras**: Bring binoculars for birdwatching and wildlife viewing, and use a zoom

lens on your camera to capture images from a safe distance.

By visiting the right spots and taking the time to observe, you'll have a rewarding experience exploring the diverse flora and fauna of Banff and Jasper National Parks. These parks are teeming with wildlife and plant species that represent the incredible biodiversity of the Canadian Rockies, offering something special for every visitor.

Guided Tours and Nature Walks

Enjoying responsible wildlife viewing is crucial for both the safety of visitors and the preservation of the animals and their habitats. Banff and Jasper National Parks are home to diverse wildlife, and it's important to observe these creatures in ways that do not disturb them or their environment. Here's a guide on how visitors can engage in responsible wildlife viewing and what tours or guides are available to enhance the experience while contributing to conservation efforts.

How to Enjoy Responsible Wildlife Viewing Without Disturbing Animals

1. Keep a Safe Distance

One of the most important aspects of responsible wildlife viewing is maintaining a safe distance from the animals. This ensures that they can go about their natural behaviors without feeling threatened or stressed.

- **Guidelines**: Parks Canada recommends staying at least 30 meters (100 feet) away from larger animals like deer and elk, and at least 100 meters (300 feet) from bears, wolves, and cougars. This prevents the animals from becoming habituated to humans, which can be dangerous for both visitors and the wildlife.
- **Use Binoculars and Zoom Lenses**: To observe wildlife without disturbing them, it's best to bring binoculars or a camera with a zoom lens. This allows you to watch the animals closely without getting too close physically. For example, binoculars are ideal

for spotting bighorn sheep on rocky cliffs or bears foraging in the distance.

2. Don't Feed or Approach Wildlife

Feeding wildlife, whether intentionally or accidentally, is harmful to the animals and illegal in the national parks. Human food can cause animals to become dependent on it, altering their natural foraging behaviors and leading them into conflict with humans.

- **Keep Food Stored Properly**: Whether camping or hiking, always store food in animal-proof containers or your vehicle. Never leave food scraps or litter behind, as this can attract animals to areas frequented by humans, increasing the risk of encounters.

- **Respect Animal Space**: Even if animals seem calm, such as elk grazing in an open field, resist the temptation to approach them. Animals, especially during mating season or when protecting their young, can become aggressive if they feel threatened.

3. Stay on Designated Trails

Many species in Banff and Jasper are sensitive to human presence, particularly when visitors stray from designated trails. Staying on marked paths helps protect both the animals and their habitats.

- **Why it Matters**: Walking off-trail can disturb ground-nesting birds, damage fragile vegetation, and disrupt wildlife in critical feeding or breeding areas. For example, certain wildflowers in alpine meadows are highly sensitive to foot traffic, and trampling these plants can cause long-term damage to the ecosystem.

- **Use Guided Tours for Backcountry Access**: If you're interested in exploring more remote areas of the parks, consider joining a guided tour. Professional guides ensure that you stick to eco-friendly practices, reducing your impact on the environment.

4. Watch for Signs of Distress

If an animal appears agitated or changes its behavior because of your presence—such as moving away, vocalizing, or looking directly at you—it's time to back off. Respecting their space ensures the animal doesn't feel the need to defend itself or its territory.

- **Understanding Animal Signals**: Wildlife like elk or deer might signal agitation by stomping their feet or moving toward you. Bears may "bluff charge" if they feel cornered. Recognizing these signs can help prevent dangerous situations while also protecting the animal from stress.

Tours and Guides for Learning About the Parks' Ecosystems and Conservation

Guided tours offer a fantastic way to learn about the rich ecosystems of Banff and Jasper while ensuring responsible wildlife viewing. Many tour operators in these parks emphasize environmental education and conservation, allowing visitors to experience the parks in a sustainable way.

1. Parks Canada Interpretive Programs

Parks Canada offers a range of interpretive programs that educate visitors about the flora, fauna, and ecosystems in both Banff and Jasper. These programs are led by knowledgeable park guides who explain the importance of conservation and how to engage responsibly with the natural environment.

- **Programs Available**: Some of the most popular programs include guided hikes, wildlife talks, and interactive exhibits. These are great for families or visitors looking to deepen their understanding of the natural world.
- **Contribution to Conservation**: By participating in these programs, visitors help support the ongoing conservation efforts of Parks Canada, as the revenue from these programs goes back into maintaining the parks and protecting their ecosystems.

2. Guided Wildlife Tours

Numerous companies offer specialized wildlife tours that focus on spotting animals like grizzly bears, elk, and wolves while maintaining a responsible and ethical distance.

- **Top Providers**:
    - **Great Divide Nature Interpretation** in Banff offers small group wildlife tours that take visitors to key wildlife corridors while educating them about the animals' behaviors, habitats, and conservation status.
    - **Jasper Wildlife Tours** provides guided tours in areas where animals like moose, bears, and

wolves are commonly sighted. These tours often take place early in the morning or late in the evening when wildlife is most active.

- **Contribution to Conservation**: These tours are designed with conservation in mind. Professional guides often contribute to citizen science projects by documenting wildlife sightings, which helps with the parks' monitoring efforts. Additionally, some tour companies donate a portion of their proceeds to wildlife conservation initiatives.

3. Glacier Tours and Eco-Tours

In Jasper, the **Columbia Icefield Glacier Adventure** offers a unique opportunity to walk on the **Athabasca Glacier** while learning about the effects of climate change on glaciers. The tour guides explain the significance of the icefields and the role they play in maintaining the region's water systems.

- **Contribution to Conservation**: These tours emphasize the importance of reducing human impact on fragile ecosystems like glaciers. Visitors learn about how small actions, like reducing plastic waste and minimizing carbon footprints, can contribute to the long-term health of these natural wonders.

4. Canoe and Kayak Eco-Tours

Water-based tours, such as canoe and kayak eco-tours on **Maligne Lake** or **Lake Minnewanka**, offer a peaceful way to observe wildlife while learning about aquatic ecosystems.

- **What to Expect**: These tours often highlight how the lakes were formed by glaciers and discuss the native fish species and birds that thrive in these waters.

Experienced guides share insights into the importance of maintaining the health of these freshwater systems.

- **Contribution to Conservation**: Eco-tours are designed to minimize impact on the environment. By using non-motorized boats and following strict "leave no trace" principles, these tours ensure the ecosystems are preserved for future generations

Final Thoughts for Responsible Wildlife Viewing and Eco-Tourism

By practicing responsible wildlife viewing and participating in guided tours focused on conservation, visitors to Banff and Jasper can enjoy unforgettable experiences without disrupting the delicate balance of these ecosystems. The educational aspect of these tours also plays a key role in raising awareness about the importance of protecting natural environments, ensuring that future generations can continue to appreciate the beauty of the Canadian Rockies.

Chapter 10

Dining in the Rockies Best Food and Drink Options.

Dining in the Canadian Rockies is a memorable experience, offering a mix of local flavors, international cuisine, and dishes inspired by the rugged beauty of the landscape. In Banff and Jasper, you'll find everything from fine dining establishments serving gourmet meals to cozy mountain cafés with homey atmospheres. Here's a guide to the best food and drink options in both Banff and Jasper, including restaurant addresses, locations, and a peek into the kind of cuisine they offer.

Best Dining Options in Banff

1. The Bison Restaurant

- **Location**: 211 Bear St #213, Banff, AB T1L 1A1
- **Cuisine**: Contemporary Canadian
- **Description**: The Bison is a favorite among locals and visitors alike, known for its focus on locally sourced ingredients and seasonal dishes. The menu is a celebration of Canadian cuisine, featuring dishes like bison short ribs, wild-caught fish, and locally sourced vegetables. In the summer, the rooftop patio offers stunning views of the surrounding mountains.
    - **Must-Try Dishes**: Bison tartare, elk poutine, and Alberta lamb shank.
    - **Atmosphere**: The Bison blends rustic charm with a contemporary, upscale feel. It's perfect for a special evening out with friends or a romantic dinner.

2. Park Distillery Restaurant and Bar

- **Location**: 219 Banff Ave, Banff, AB T1L 1B2
- **Cuisine**: Canadian, Smokehouse
- **Description**: Located on the bustling Banff Avenue, Park Distillery is a unique spot that combines a craft distillery with a casual, rustic eatery. They serve campfire-inspired dishes cooked over open flames, offering a true taste of the Rockies. The restaurant distills its own spirits on-site, so you can enjoy house-made gin, vodka, and whiskey with your meal.

- **Must-Try Dishes**: Rotisserie chicken, campfire plank salmon, and their signature cocktails made with house-distilled spirits.
- **Atmosphere**: Warm, casual, and lively, with an emphasis on locally sourced ingredients and a true mountain vibe.

3. The Grizzly House

- **Location**: 207 Banff Ave, Banff, AB T1L 1B4
- **Cuisine**: Fondue, Steakhouse
- **Description**: A Banff institution since the 1960s, The Grizzly House offers a unique dining experience with its selection of fondue dishes. You can cook your own food at the table, choosing from a variety of meats (including exotic options like shark or buffalo) and cheeses. It's an interactive and fun way to dine, perfect for groups or adventurous eaters.
  - **Must-Try Dishes**: The Fondue Experience (try a mix of cheese, meat, and chocolate fondues), buffalo steak.
  - **Atmosphere**: Rustic, cozy, and a bit quirky, with an old-school feel that brings you back to Banff's early tourism days.

4. Sky Bistro

- **Location**: 1 Mountain Ave, Banff, AB T1L 1J3 (Top of Banff Gondola)
- **Cuisine**: Canadian, Fine Dining
- **Description**: Located at the summit of Sulphur Mountain, Sky Bistro offers not only amazing food

but also some of the most breathtaking views in Banff. The menu focuses on regional Canadian cuisine, with ingredients sourced from Alberta and British Columbia. The journey to the restaurant via the Banff Gondola only adds to the experience.

- o **Must-Try Dishes**: Alberta beef tenderloin, West Coast seafood chowder, and their famous bison burger.
- o **Atmosphere**: Upscale, modern, and unforgettable, especially with the panoramic mountain views that surround you.

Best Dining Options in Jasper

1. Jasper Brewing Company

- **Location**: 624 Connaught Dr, Jasper, AB T0E 1E0
- **Cuisine**: Pub, Canadian
- **Description**: As Canada's first national park brewery, Jasper Brewing Company is a must-visit for anyone who loves craft beer and hearty pub fare. They serve a variety of local brews, all crafted in-house, alongside a menu of classic Canadian comfort food like burgers, poutine, and steaks.
    - o **Must-Try Dishes**: The Rocky Mountain Burger, elk meatloaf, and their signature craft beers (try the Jasper the Bear Ale).
    - o **Atmosphere**: Casual, lively, and perfect for an after-hike meal or a night out with friends.

2. Fiddle River Restaurant

- **Location**: 620 Connaught Dr, Jasper, AB T0E 1E0
- **Cuisine**: Seafood, Canadian
- **Description**: Known for its fresh seafood and stunning views of the Athabasca River, Fiddle River is one of the top dining destinations in Jasper. The restaurant focuses on sustainable seafood options, along with local game and farm-to-table ingredients.
    - **Must-Try Dishes**: Cedar plank salmon, Alaskan king crab, and their wild game trio (which can include bison, elk, and venison).
    - **Atmosphere**: Cozy, intimate, with large windows that give you a perfect view of the Rockies while you enjoy your meal.

3. The Pines Restaurant

- **Location**: 6 Pyramid Lake Rd, Jasper, AB T0E 1E0
- **Cuisine**: Canadian, Fine Dining
- **Description**: Located in the Pyramid Lake Resort, The Pines offers refined Canadian cuisine with a focus on locally sourced ingredients. The restaurant is known for its elegant presentations and stunning lakeside location, making it a great spot for a romantic dinner or a special occasion.
    - **Must-Try Dishes**: Alberta beef ribeye, wild boar rack, and their decadent desserts like sticky toffee pudding.

- o **Atmosphere**: Upscale, serene, and perfect for enjoying a meal with panoramic views of Pyramid Lake and the surrounding peaks.

4. Evil Dave's Grill

- **Location**: 622 Patricia St, Jasper, AB T0E 1E0
- **Cuisine**: Contemporary, Canadian
- **Description**: Evil Dave's Grill is known for its creative twist on Canadian dishes, blending international flavors with locally sourced ingredients. The quirky atmosphere and bold flavors make it a favorite among Jasper visitors. The menu changes seasonally to highlight the freshest ingredients.
  - o **Must-Try Dishes**: The Malicious Salmon (blackened salmon with a mango sauce), Hell's Chicken (spicy, Asian-inspired dish), and their wicked chocolate cake for dessert.
  - o **Atmosphere**: Fun, funky, and unpretentious, making it great for anyone looking for a casual yet flavorful dining experience.

Cafés and Casual Eateries

1. Wild Flour Bakery (Banff)

- **Location**: 211 Bear St, Banff, AB T1L 1B8
- **Cuisine**: Café, Bakery

- **Description**: A great spot for breakfast or a light lunch, Wild Flour Bakery is known for its artisan breads, pastries, and strong, locally roasted coffee. It's a cozy place to stop before a day of hiking, with grab-and-go options like sandwiches and salads.
    - **Must-Try Dishes**: Almond croissant, sourdough bread, and their vegan power bowls.
    - **Atmosphere**: Casual, relaxed, with a community vibe.

2. Bear's Paw Bakery (Jasper)

- **Location**: 4 Pyramid Lake Rd, Jasper, AB T0E 1E0
- **Cuisine**: Café, Bakery
- **Description**: A local institution, Bear's Paw Bakery is beloved for its fresh pastries, baked goods, and strong coffee. Perfect for a quick breakfast before hitting the trails or for grabbing a sweet treat after a long hike, this cozy bakery is a favorite among both locals and visitors.
    - **Must-Try Dishes**: Sticky cinnamon buns, raspberry white chocolate scones, and their signature coffee blends.
    - **Atmosphere**: Warm and welcoming, with a rustic mountain feel.

Tips for Enjoying Dining in Banff and Jasper

- **Make Reservations**: Many of the more popular restaurants, particularly during peak tourist season (June through September), fill up quickly, so it's a good idea to make reservations, especially for dinner.

- **Local Ingredients**: Many restaurants in Banff and Jasper focus on farm-to-table dining, with menus that change seasonally to highlight local ingredients. Look for game meats like bison, elk, and venison, as well as wild-caught fish from nearby waters.

- **Cafés for a Quick Bite**: Both towns have a variety of great bakeries and cafés that are perfect for breakfast or lunch on the go, especially if you have a day of outdoor adventure ahead of you.

Whether you're looking for a casual bite or an upscale dining experience, Banff and Jasper offer some of the best food options in the Rockies, combining local flavors with the beauty of the surrounding wilderness.

Picnic Spots with Stunning Views in Banff and Jasper

Both Banff and Jasper National Parks offer numerous scenic spots where visitors can enjoy packed meals surrounded by the breathtaking beauty of the Canadian Rockies. Here are some of the best picnic areas with incredible views.

1. Lake Minnewanka Picnic Area (Banff)

- **Location**: Just a 10-minute drive from Banff townsite, Lake Minnewanka is one of the most accessible and scenic spots for a picnic.
- **What to Expect**: This large glacial lake is surrounded by towering mountains, offering gorgeous views while you enjoy your meal. The area has plenty of picnic tables, and it's also close to several easy hiking trails if you want to stretch your legs before or after your meal. The shimmering blue water and surrounding peaks make it a top spot for photographers as well.
    - **Amenities**: Picnic tables, fire pits, restrooms, and parking are available on-site.

2. Pyramid Lake Picnic Area (Jasper)

- **Location**: Just a short drive from Jasper townsite, Pyramid Lake is a serene spot for a peaceful picnic.
- **What to Expect**: The view of **Pyramid Mountain** reflecting on the calm waters of the lake is

unforgettable. The picnic areas are well-spaced, providing privacy, and the site also offers hiking and canoeing options. **Pyramid Island** is another great spot within walking distance for a picnic, accessible via a short walk over a wooden footbridge.

- o **Amenities**: Picnic tables, restrooms, and watercraft rentals are available. You can also rent kayaks or paddleboats nearby.

3. Johnston Canyon Picnic Area (Banff)

- **Location**: Along the **Bow Valley Parkway**, approximately 25 kilometers from Banff townsite.
- **What to Expect**: This popular picnic area is located near the trailhead for the **Johnston Canyon** hike, one of Banff's most scenic and family-friendly hikes. After a morning hike to the Lower or Upper Falls, you can relax and enjoy your lunch surrounded by forests and the sound of the nearby creek. The area is shaded, providing a cool retreat during the summer months.
  - o **Amenities**: Picnic tables, restrooms, and parking. The nearby **Johnston Canyon Lodge and Bungalows** offer snack options if you haven't packed a meal.

4. Edith Cavell Meadows Picnic Area (Jasper)

- **Location**: Close to the **Mount Edith Cavell** trailhead, about 30 kilometers from Jasper townsite.
- **What to Expect**: This picnic area offers some of the most dramatic views in Jasper, with **Mount Edith Cavell** towering overhead. The site provides a

peaceful atmosphere, perfect for enjoying your packed meal after a hike to **Cavell Glacier** or **Angel Glacier**. It's a less crowded area, so you can often enjoy the beauty of the place with minimal disturbance.

- o **Amenities**: Picnic tables, restrooms, and parking.

5. Tunnel Mountain Reservoir (Banff)

- **Location**: A short drive or walk from Banff townsite, Tunnel Mountain offers elevated views of the surrounding mountains and valleys.

- **What to Expect**: This grassy picnic area provides stunning panoramic views of **Mount Rundle**, **Sulphur Mountain**, and the **Bow River**. It's a quieter spot compared to other picnic areas closer to town, offering a tranquil escape with plenty of space for a relaxing meal.

  - o **Amenities**: Picnic tables, restrooms, and parking.

Sustainable or Eco-Friendly Dining Options in Banff and Jasper

Many restaurants in Banff and Jasper have embraced sustainable practices to minimize their environmental impact while offering delicious, eco-friendly meals. Here are some top choices for sustainable dining:

1. Nourish Bistro (Banff)

- **Location**: 211 Bear St #110, Banff, AB T1L 1A1
- **Sustainability Practices**: Nourish Bistro is a popular vegetarian and vegan restaurant focused on sustainability. They source organic, local ingredients wherever possible and offer creative plant-based dishes with minimal environmental impact. The restaurant also prioritizes waste reduction and responsible sourcing.
    - **Menu Highlights**: The Buddha bowl, wild mushroom risotto, and their signature nachos, which are packed with over 27 ingredients.
    - **Eco-Friendly Initiatives**: Use of biodegradable packaging, locally sourced produce, and a commitment to reducing food waste.

2. The Juniper Bistro (Banff)

- **Location**: 1 Juniper Way, Banff, AB T1L 1E1
- **Sustainability Practices**: Located in the Juniper Hotel, this restaurant is known for its stunning views

and commitment to sustainable dining. The Juniper Bistro sources ingredients locally, supports regional farmers, and works to minimize its carbon footprint. They serve contemporary Canadian cuisine using wild game, seasonal vegetables, and ethically sourced seafood.

- o **Menu Highlights**: Bison short ribs, smoked trout, and farm-fresh vegetables.
- o **Eco-Friendly Initiatives**: Locally sourced ingredients, energy-efficient kitchen practices, and partnerships with nearby organic farms.

3. Tekarra Restaurant (Jasper)

- **Location**: 57 Sleepy Hollow Rd, Jasper, AB T0E 1E0
- **Sustainability Practices**: Tekarra Restaurant is deeply committed to sustainability, focusing on local and organic produce, as well as wild game and sustainably caught seafood. They also participate in composting and recycling efforts to minimize waste. The restaurant's menu is designed around seasonal availability, so it changes throughout the year to reflect the freshest ingredients.
  - o **Menu Highlights**: Wild game terrine, elk tenderloin, and vegetable terrine.
  - o **Eco-Friendly Initiatives**: Sourcing from local, sustainable farms, and a commitment to composting and waste reduction.

4. The Raven Bistro (Jasper)

- **Location**: 504 Patricia St, Jasper, AB T0E 1E0
- **Sustainability Practices**: The Raven Bistro emphasizes the use of organic, locally sourced, and sustainably farmed ingredients. Known for its fusion of Mediterranean and Canadian flavors, The Raven Bistro offers vegan and vegetarian options that cater to eco-conscious diners. Their dishes are crafted with minimal waste and environmentally friendly methods.
    - **Menu Highlights**: The Moroccan-inspired lamb tagine, vegan chickpea fries, and roasted vegetable quinoa salad.
    - **Eco-Friendly Initiatives**: Reducing single-use plastics, using compostable packaging, and sourcing from regional farms and suppliers.

5. The Spice Joint (Jasper)

- **Location**: 622 Patricia St, Jasper, AB T0E 1E0
- **Sustainability Practices**: This small, locally owned restaurant focuses on Jamaican-inspired cuisine with a commitment to sustainability. The Spice Joint uses locally grown ingredients when possible and has a waste-reduction program in place. They aim to minimize their carbon footprint by using eco-friendly packaging and focusing on plant-based options.

- **Menu Highlights**: Jerk chicken wraps, vegan bowls, and Jamaican patties.

- **Eco-Friendly Initiatives**: Compostable takeout containers, minimizing food waste, and offering a variety of plant-based options to reduce environmental impact.

Tips for Eco-Friendly Dining in the Rockies

- **Bring Your Own Reusable Items**: If you're packing your own meals for a picnic or ordering takeout, consider bringing reusable utensils, water bottles, and containers to minimize single-use plastic waste.

- **Support Local**: Choose restaurants and cafés that prioritize local, organic ingredients. This not only reduces the carbon footprint associated with transporting food but also supports local farmers and producers.

- **Opt for Plant-Based Meals**: Plant-based meals typically have a lower environmental impact compared to those centered around meat and dairy. Many restaurants in Banff and Jasper now offer delicious vegan and vegetarian options.

Dining in Banff and Jasper can be a sustainable and environmentally conscious experience, with many establishments focusing on eco-friendly practices. Whether you're enjoying a picnic at a scenic spot or dining at a local bistro, you can savor the flavors of the Rockies while contributing to the preservation of these beautiful national parks.

Chapter 11

Safety Tips for Outdoor Exploration

When exploring Banff and Jasper National Parks, visitors need to be mindful of safety, especially in areas where encounters with wildlife like bears, elk, and other animals are common. These tips will help you stay safe in bear country and when encountering other wildlife.

Safety Tips for Bear Country

1. Carry Bear Spray (And Know How to Use It)

Bear spray is one of the most important tools for staying safe in bear country. It can deter an aggressive bear if used correctly and is recommended for all hikers and campers.

- **What to Do**: Always carry bear spray in an easily accessible spot (like on your belt or backpack strap). Make sure to know how to use it—practice removing the safety clip and aiming the canister. Spray should be deployed when the bear is within 10 to 30 feet, aiming for the bear's face.

2. Make Noise

Bears, especially grizzlies, tend to avoid humans when they are aware of their presence. To reduce the risk of surprising a bear, make plenty of noise while hiking, especially in dense forest or near streams where the sound of your approach may be muffled.

- **What to Do**: Talk loudly, clap your hands, or use a bear bell. Travel in groups, as larger groups make more noise naturally, and are less likely to surprise a bear. Solo hikers are at a higher risk of bear encounters

3. Stay on Marked Trails

Bears tend to avoid heavily trafficked areas. Staying on marked and well-traveled trails reduces the risk of coming across a bear unexpectedly. Avoid hiking through dense bushes or off-trail areas where bears may be foraging.

4. Store Food Properly

Food and strong-smelling items attract bears, so proper food storage is key in bear country, especially when camping.

- **What to Do**: Use bear-proof food storage lockers or hang your food in a tree, away from your sleeping area. Keep all food, trash, and scented items (toiletries) secured. Never store food in your tent.

5. Know What to Do if You Encounter a Bear

- **If You See a Bear From a Distance**: Stay calm, back away slowly, and do not run. Running can trigger a bear's chase instinct.

- **If a Bear Approaches You**: Speak in a calm voice, wave your arms, and try to make yourself appear larger. Do not turn your back on the bear. If the bear continues to approach, prepare to use bear spray.

- **If a Bear Charges**: Remain calm. Bears sometimes "bluff charge" to intimidate. Stand your ground and deploy bear spray if the bear is within range. In a rare attack, play dead if it's a grizzly bear or fight back if it's a black bear.

Safety Tips for Other Wildlife Encounters

1. Keep a Safe Distance

Maintaining a safe distance from all wildlife is essential. Elk, moose, and bighorn sheep may look docile, but they can be dangerous if they feel threatened.

- **What to Do**: Parks Canada recommends keeping at least 30 meters (100 feet) away from large animals like elk and moose, and 100 meters (330 feet) from bears and wolves. Use binoculars or a zoom lens for closer views without approaching.

2. Stay Calm During Encounters

If you unexpectedly come across an animal, stay calm and avoid sudden movements. Slowly back away without turning your back, and give the animal plenty of space to move.

3. Be Cautious During Mating or Calving Seasons

Certain animals, like elk and deer, can become especially aggressive during mating season (fall) or when protecting their young (spring).

- **What to Do**: Avoid areas known for wildlife activity during these times, or take extra precautions. For example, elk may charge if they feel their territory or young are threatened.

4. Use Wildlife Corridors Safely

When driving in Banff and Jasper, be mindful of wildlife corridors, especially at dawn or dusk when animals are more active.

- **What to Do**: Drive slowly and be alert for animals crossing the road. Collisions with wildlife can be dangerous for both animals and people, so be vigilant, especially in areas with wildlife warning signs.

Tours and Guides for Safe Wildlife Viewing

Joining a guided wildlife tour in Banff or Jasper can enhance your wildlife experience while ensuring your safety and contributing to conservation efforts. Professional guides know where animals are most likely to be seen and can help interpret animal behavior, providing a safe and responsible way to enjoy the parks.

- **Popular Guided Wildlife Tours**:

Jasper Wildlife Tours: These tours take you into wildlife-rich areas of Jasper, offering opportunities to see elk, deer, bears, and other animals while educating visitors about safety and conservation.

Banff Wildlife Tours: Companies like **Discover Banff Tours** provide educational and safe wildlife viewing experiences, focusing on bear safety and local ecosystems

Navigating Trails Safely in Banff and Jasper.

Exploring the trails of Banff and Jasper National Parks offers a great way to experience the natural beauty of the Rockies, but it's essential to navigate them safely and be prepared for potential hazards. Here's how you can stay safe and avoid common dangers while hiking, along with available emergency resources.

How to Navigate the Trails

1. Use a Physical Map and GPS

Cell service can be unreliable in many areas of the parks, especially in remote backcountry regions. Relying solely on your phone for navigation can be risky. It's important to carry a physical map, such as those available at visitor centers, and know how to read it.

- **Recommended Maps**: National Topographic System maps or the popular **Gem Trek** maps, which detail the most-used trails in Banff and Jasper.

- **GPS and Navigation Tools**: If you're venturing into more remote areas, consider bringing a handheld GPS device for backup, especially if you're unfamiliar with the terrain.

2. Stick to Marked Trails

One of the most important safety tips is to stay on the designated trails. Wandering off marked paths can lead to disorientation, encounters with wildlife, or exposure to dangerous terrain such as loose rocks or steep drop-offs.

- **Why It Matters**: Staying on the trail protects both you and the environment. Off-trail hiking can damage delicate vegetation and disturb wildlife habitats.

3. Monitor the Weather

Weather in the Canadian Rockies is notoriously unpredictable and can change rapidly, especially at higher elevations. A clear day can quickly turn into a stormy afternoon with rain, snow, or strong winds, even in the summer.

- **What to Do**: Always check the weather forecast before heading out and be prepared for sudden changes. If you're hiking at higher altitudes, bring layers, including a waterproof jacket, and be aware that temperature drops and snowstorms can occur even in July or August.

4. Know the Signs and Trail Markers

Both Banff and Jasper use consistent trail markers and signs to guide hikers. Understanding these signs is crucial for staying on the right path.

- **Trail Markers**: Look for markers on trees, rocks, or posts that indicate the trail's difficulty, distance, and direction. Pay attention to warnings about potential hazards, such as steep sections or wildlife sightings.

Common Hazards to Avoid

1. Weather Changes

Rapid weather changes can pose significant risks to hikers, especially at higher elevations where snowstorms or cold winds can catch hikers off guard.

- **How to Prepare**: Carry extra layers, including a warm jacket, gloves, and hat. Always have a waterproof outer layer and consider bringing a thermal blanket for emergencies. If you notice ominous clouds or rapid temperature drops, turn back or seek shelter immediately.

2. Slippery Terrain and Loose Rocks

Many trails in Banff and Jasper involve hiking over uneven or rocky terrain, especially on steeper trails like **Sulphur Skyline** or **Wilcox Pass**. Wet or icy conditions can make these paths treacherous.

- **How to Prepare**: Wear sturdy, waterproof hiking boots with good grip. Trekking poles can also help stabilize your footing on steep or slippery trails. Be cautious when crossing rocky areas, and avoid climbing over loose boulders that could shift under your weight.

3. Creek and River Crossings

Some trails, especially in spring and early summer when snowmelt is high, may require crossing creeks or rivers. Fast-flowing water can be dangerous and cold, and slippery rocks add to the risk.

- **What to Do**: Cross only at designated areas, and avoid crossing if the water level seems high or the current is strong. If unsure, turn back or find an alternative route. If you must cross, unbuckle your backpack so you can quickly remove it in an emergency, and use trekking poles for balance.

4. Altitude Sickness

If you're hiking at high elevations, such as **Parker Ridge** or **Wilcox Pass**, altitude sickness can affect some hikers, causing dizziness, shortness of breath, and fatigue.

- **How to Prepare**: Ascend slowly to give your body time to adjust. Drink plenty of water, and rest frequently if you start feeling unwell. If symptoms worsen, descend to a lower altitude as quickly as possible.

Emergency Resources and Preparation for Medical or Natural Emergencies

1. Know Emergency Contact Information

If you encounter an emergency in Banff or Jasper, being able to quickly contact the right people is crucial. Make sure you know the emergency numbers and have access to communication.

- **Emergency Contacts**:
    - In an emergency, dial **911**. Both parks have emergency responders for medical, fire, or search and rescue situations.
    - Park-specific help can also be reached through Parks Canada by calling **1-877-852-3100** for non-life-threatening emergencies, such as getting lost or encountering dangerous conditions.

2. Carry a First-Aid Kit

A well-stocked first-aid kit can make a huge difference in the event of an injury, especially if you're far from help. Make sure your kit includes:

- Bandages, gauze, antiseptic wipes
- Blister care (such as moleskin or blister bandages)
- Pain relievers (ibuprofen or acetaminophen)
- Tweezers, scissors, and a small emergency blanket

3. Download Offline Maps

As cell service is unreliable in many areas of Banff and Jasper, having offline maps downloaded on your phone or GPS device is essential. Apps like **AllTrails** or **Gaia GPS** allow you to download trail maps that can be used without internet connectivity.

- **Tip**: Always tell someone your hiking route and expected return time before you leave, especially if you're exploring remote areas.

4. Avalanche Safety in Winter

If you're hiking or skiing in winter, be aware of avalanche risks, especially in higher elevations.

- **What to Do**: Check the avalanche forecast for the area before setting out. If traveling through avalanche-prone terrain, carry an avalanche beacon, probe, and shovel, and know how to use them. Consider joining a guided tour or taking an avalanche safety course before heading out in the backcountry.

5. Emergency Shelters

Some backcountry trails have emergency shelters or huts in case of sudden weather changes or injuries. These shelters are typically basic, offering protection from the elements but limited supplies.

- **What to Know**: Locations of these shelters are marked on most detailed trail maps. However, these huts should not be relied upon as primary accommodation—only as a backup in case of emergency.

Chapter 12

Traveling with Kids in Banff and Jasper National Parks

Traveling with kids in Banff and Jasper National Parks is a fantastic experience, as these parks offer a wide range of kid-friendly activities, family-friendly accommodations, and budget-friendly dining options. Here's a comprehensive guide to help you plan your trip, ensuring that the entire family enjoys the beauty of the Canadian Rockies.

Must-Visit Spots for Families and Kids

Both Banff and Jasper offer numerous attractions that cater to families, ranging from easy hikes to educational experiences.

1. Lake Louise (Banff)

- **Location**: Lake Louise, Banff National Park, AB

Why It's Great for Kids: Lake Louise is a beautiful, easily accessible destination with calm waters perfect for families. You can rent canoes in the summer or skate on the frozen lake in the winter. The surrounding trails, like the **Lakeshore Trail**, are flat and perfect for little ones.

Booking Tip: Canoe rentals are available at the **Fairmont Chateau Lake Louise** boathouse. Book early during peak summer months.

2. Banff Gondola and Sulphur Mountain (Banff)

- **Location**: 100 Mountain Ave, Banff, AB T1L 1B2

Why It's Great for Kids: The Banff Gondola is an exciting ride that kids will love, taking you to the top of Sulphur Mountain with breathtaking views. Once at the summit, there are kid-friendly interactive exhibits at the **Above Banff Interpretive Centre** and easy boardwalks to explore.

Booking Tip: Purchase tickets online in advance, especially during the summer and fall months, to avoid long lines. The gondola operates year-round.

3. Maligne Lake and Spirit Island (Jasper)

- **Location**: 48 kilometers southeast of Jasper townsite, Jasper National Park

Why It's Great for Kids: **Maligne Lake** is one of Jasper's most famous spots. Families can enjoy boat cruises to **Spirit Island** or rent kayaks. There's plenty of space for a family picnic while admiring the lake and mountain views.

Booking Tip: Book the **Maligne Lake Cruise** in advance, particularly in the summer. Rentals for canoes and kayaks are also available at the boathouse.

4. Jasper SkyTram (Jasper)

- **Location**: Whistlers Rd, Jasper, AB T0E 1E0

Why It's Great for Kids: This aerial tramway takes you and your kids to the top of **Whistlers Mountain**. The ride is exciting, and the summit offers easy trails with incredible views. The summit is an ideal spot for families to explore, picnic, and take memorable photos.

Booking Tip: It's recommended to book tickets online, as the SkyTram gets busy during peak times (summer and fall)

5. Icefields Parkway and Athabasca Glacier (Between Banff and Jasper)

- **Location**: Accessible from the **Icefields Parkway (Highway 93)**

Why It's Great for Kids: The **Athabasca Glacier** is part of the **Columbia Icefield**, and families can take the **Glacier Adventure Tour** to explore the glacier aboard an Ice

Explorer vehicle. Kids love walking on the glacier and learning about its formation through guided tours.

Booking Tip: Book the **Glacier Adventure Tour** and the nearby **Skywalk** online in advance, as both attractions can fill up quickly during summer.

Kid-Friendly Accommodations in Banff and Jasper

Finding family-friendly accommodations in Banff and Jasper is easy, with many hotels offering amenities like spacious family suites, playgrounds, and activities for children.

1. Fairmont Chateau Lake Louise (Banff)

- **Location**: 111 Lake Louise Dr, Lake Louise, AB T0L 1E0

What Makes It Kid-Friendly: This iconic hotel offers family packages, rooms with mountain views, and kid-friendly amenities like babysitting services, children's menus, and organized outdoor activities like nature walks and canoeing.

Booking Tip: Book well in advance, especially during the summer and holiday seasons, as this hotel is highly sought after

2. Tunnel Mountain Resort (Banff)

- **Location**: 502 Tunnel Mountain Rd, Banff, AB T1L 1B1

What Makes It Kid-Friendly: Tunnel Mountain Resort offers spacious suites and cabins, many equipped with kitchens. The resort has an indoor pool, playground, and BBQ areas, making it perfect for families who want to relax and enjoy a self-catered experience.

Booking Tip: If traveling during peak seasons (summer and ski season), book several months in advance to secure a family-friendly suite.

3. Jasper Park Lodge (Jasper)

- **Location**: Old Lodge Rd, Jasper, AB T0E 1E0

What Makes It Kid-Friendly: Set on the shore of **Lac Beauvert**, the Jasper Park Lodge is a family-friendly resort offering a wide range of outdoor activities like canoeing, horseback riding, and hiking. The lodge also has a kids' activity program, perfect for keeping young travelers entertained.

Booking Tip: Opt for the family cabins for more space and privacy. Summer reservations should be made several months in advance.

4. Pyramid Lake Resort (Jasper)

- **Location**: 5 kilometers from Jasper townsite, Pyramid Lake Rd, Jasper, AB T0E 1E0

What Makes It Kid-Friendly: This lakeside resort offers family-friendly amenities, including boat rentals, a private beach, and hiking trails right outside the door. Rooms are spacious, and the location offers a serene escape while still being close to town.

Booking Tip: The resort is popular during the summer months, so early booking is recommended.

Budget-Friendly Restaurants for Families

Dining out with kids doesn't have to break the bank. Banff and Jasper have several family-friendly and budget-conscious options for a tasty meal after a day of exploring.

1. Eddie Burger + Bar (Banff)

- **Location**: 137 Banff Ave #6, Banff, AB T1L 1C8
- **Cuisine**: American, Burgers

Why It's Great for Families: Eddie Burger + Bar is a casual, family-friendly spot offering a variety of burgers, fries, and milkshakes. The restaurant has a relaxed atmosphere, and the prices are affordable, making it perfect for a quick bite with kids.

Budget-Friendly Tip: Look out for lunch specials and kids' menu items like mini-burgers and mac and cheese.

2. Patricia Street Deli (Jasper)

- **Location**: 610 Patricia St, Jasper, AB T0E 1E0
- **Cuisine**: Deli, Sandwiches

Why It's Great for Families: This small deli is a favorite among locals and visitors alike for its fresh sandwiches, wraps, and salads. It's a great option for families looking to grab a quick, healthy meal on the go. The prices are budget-friendly, and portions are generous.

Budget-Friendly Tip: Pack your picnic lunch from this deli before heading out for a family hike or a day of exploring.

3. Wild Flour Bakery (Banff)

- **Location**: 211 Bear St #110, Banff, AB T1L 1B8
- **Cuisine**: Café, Bakery

Why It's Great for Families: This cozy bakery offers affordable breakfast and lunch options, with freshly baked goods, sandwiches, and kid-friendly treats like muffins and cookies. It's a great place to stop for a quick meal before heading out on a family adventure.

Budget-Friendly Tip: The breakfast options are affordable and filling, making it a perfect spot for a budget-friendly start to the day.

4. Coco's Café (Jasper)

- **Location**: 608-B Patricia St, Jasper, AB T0E 1E0
- **Cuisine**: Café, Vegetarian-Friendly

Why It's Great for Families: Coco's Café is a casual, family-friendly spot offering a variety of affordable breakfast and lunch items. It's known for its hearty sandwiches, soups, and baked goods, making it a great stop for families looking for fresh, homemade food.

Budget-Friendly Tip: The café has several vegetarian and gluten-free options, which cater well to families with dietary restrictions.

Tips for Traveling with Kids in Banff and Jasper

- **Plan Ahead**: Both Banff and Jasper are popular destinations, and accommodations and tours can fill up quickly, especially in the summer. Booking months in advance ensures you have access to the best family-friendly options.

- **Pack Layers**: The weather in the Canadian Rockies can change quickly, so make sure to pack layers, even in summer. Kids may get cold on high-altitude hikes or boat rides.

- **Bring Snacks**: Some activities, like hiking or scenic drives, may take longer than expected. Having snacks on hand can help keep kids happy and energized during longer adventures.

By visiting the kid-friendly spots and enjoying family-oriented accommodations and restaurants, you can make the most of your trip to Banff and Jasper

Budget-friendly restaurants

budget-friendly restaurants in Banff and Jasper that offer great food options for families or those traveling on a budget:

Budget-Friendly Restaurants in Banff

1. Eddie Burger + Bar

- **Location**: 137 Banff Ave #6, Banff, AB T1L 1C8
- **Cuisine**: American, Burgers
- **Why It's Budget-Friendly**: Eddie Burger + Bar offers a variety of affordable burgers, fries, and shakes, making it a popular spot for families and casual diners. With menu items like classic cheeseburgers and indulgent poutines, it's an excellent choice for a tasty, satisfying meal without breaking the bank.
- **Price Range**: $10–$20 per person.
- **Tip**: Check out their daily specials or happy hour for even more savings.

2. Bear Street Tavern

- **Location**: 211 Bear St, Banff, AB T1L 1E4
- **Cuisine**: Pizza, Pub Fare
- **Why It's Budget-Friendly**: Known for its casual atmosphere and delicious wood-fired pizzas, Bear Street Tavern is a favorite among budget-conscious travelers. The portions are generous, making it

perfect for sharing with family or friends. Their pizza specials and happy hour deals provide great value for money.

- **Price Range**: $12–$25 per person.
- **Tip**: Try their signature pizzas and make sure to pair it with the in-house spicy honey sauce.

3. Tooloulou's

- **Location**: 204 Caribou St, Banff, AB T1L 1C3
- **Cuisine**: Cajun, Canadian, Breakfast
- **Why It's Budget-Friendly**: Tooloulou's is famous for its big breakfasts and Cajun-inspired dishes at very reasonable prices. This cozy spot offers a mix of North American comfort food and Louisiana specialties like gumbo and jambalaya. Their breakfast menu, featuring pancakes, waffles, and omelets, is especially popular and affordable.
- **Price Range**: $10–$20 per person.
- **Tip**: Go for their breakfast combo deals for great value.

4. Masala Authentic Indian Cuisine

- **Location**: 229 Bear St, Banff, AB T1L 1A1
- **Cuisine**: Indian
- **Why It's Budget-Friendly**: Masala offers flavorful, authentic Indian dishes in large portions, perfect for

sharing. Their selection of curries, naan, and rice dishes are budget-friendly, with plenty of vegetarian and vegan options. It's a great option for a warm, hearty meal that won't hurt your wallet.

- **Price Range**: $12–$22 per person.
- **Tip**: Try the lunch specials for extra savings.

Budget-Friendly Restaurants in Jasper

1. Patricia Street Deli

- **Location**: 610 Patricia St, Jasper, AB T0E 1E0
- **Cuisine**: Deli, Sandwiches
- **Why It's Budget-Friendly**: A go-to spot for quick and delicious sandwiches, wraps, and salads, Patricia Street Deli offers healthy and filling meals at affordable prices. You can customize your sandwiches with a variety of fresh ingredients, and the portions are perfect for an on-the-go meal while exploring Jasper.
- **Price Range**: $7–$12 per person.
- **Tip**: Grab sandwiches to take along on your hikes or for a picnic.

2. The Other Paw Bakery Café

- **Location**: 610 Connaught Dr, Jasper, AB T0E 1E0
- **Cuisine**: Café, Bakery

- **Why It's Budget-Friendly**: The Other Paw Bakery Café offers a selection of freshly baked goods, sandwiches, and soups. It's a budget-friendly option for breakfast or lunch, with delicious baked treats like scones, cookies, and muffins. Their coffee is also highly rated, making it a great stop for a quick snack.
- **Price Range**: $5–$12 per person.
- **Tip**: Check out their combo meals, which include soup, salad, or sandwich with a dessert and coffee.

3. Jasper Pizza Place

- **Location**: 402 Connaught Dr, Jasper, AB T0E 1E0
- **Cuisine**: Pizza, Italian
- **Why It's Budget-Friendly**: Jasper Pizza Place offers classic, wood-fired pizzas that are reasonably priced and perfect for families or groups. The relaxed setting and large portions make it a great spot for budget-conscious travelers. They also offer a variety of pasta dishes and salads.
- **Price Range**: $12–$20 per person.
- **Tip**: Their pizza deals for groups or families offer excellent value.

4. Lou Lou's Pizzeria

- **Location**: 407 Patricia St, Jasper, AB T0E 1E0
- **Cuisine**: Pizza, Italian

- **Why It's Budget-Friendly**: Lou Lou's Pizzeria is a casual, family-friendly restaurant offering pizza, pasta, and comfort food at great prices. The portions are generous, and their classic pizza recipes are popular with both locals and tourists. It's a perfect stop for families looking for a quick, filling meal.
- **Price Range**: $10–$18 per person.
- **Tip**: They have pizza slice deals for those looking for a quick snack.

Tips for Dining on a Budget

- **Look for Lunch Specials**: Many restaurants in Banff and Jasper offer lunch specials or happy hour deals that provide great value. These are often significantly cheaper than dinner prices but offer the same high-quality food.
- **Pack a Picnic**: With both towns offering excellent delis and bakeries, grabbing a picnic to take to one of the scenic spots in the parks is not only affordable but also allows you to enjoy the stunning views while dining.
- **Stick to Casual Dining**: Casual eateries, cafés, and pubs typically offer larger portions at more affordable prices compared to fine dining restaurants. These spots are perfect for families or those looking to save while still enjoying delicious meals.

Safety Information for Traveling with Kids in Banff and Jasper

Traveling with children to Banff and Jasper National Parks can be an incredible experience filled with outdoor adventures. However, it's essential to be well-prepared to ensure a safe and enjoyable trip. Here's a comprehensive guide on what to bring, important safety tips, and the required travel documents when exploring these stunning destinations with your kids.

What to Bring for Kids

1. Layers of Clothing

The weather in the Canadian Rockies can be unpredictable, even in summer. Temperatures can change quickly, and it's not uncommon for cool mornings to turn into warm afternoons. Layering is key when traveling with kids to keep them comfortable and prepared for any weather conditions.

- **What to Pack**:
  - **Base Layers**: Long-sleeve shirts or thermal tops to keep warm.
  - **Fleece or Sweaters**: Perfect for chilly mornings or evenings.
  - **Waterproof Jacket**: Both Banff and Jasper can see rain or sudden weather changes, so a good waterproof jacket is a must.
  - **Hats and Gloves**: Even in summer, higher elevations can get cold, so pack warm accessories for hikes or sightseeing at high altitudes.

2. Comfortable Footwear

Kids are likely to be walking or running around quite a bit, so having comfortable, sturdy footwear is crucial. Choose hiking shoes or sneakers that offer good support and grip.

- **Pro Tip**: Waterproof shoes or boots are ideal if you're planning on exploring lakes, streams, or potentially muddy trails.

3. Snacks and Water

Keeping kids hydrated and energized is important during outdoor adventures. Pack easy, healthy snacks like fruit, granola bars, and nuts. Water is essential, so bring refillable bottles to keep everyone hydrated. In Banff and Jasper, you can fill bottles at visitor centers or cafes.

4. Sun Protection

With higher elevations in both Banff and Jasper, the sun can be intense even when it feels cool. Protect your kids from UV rays by packing:

- Sunscreen (SPF 30 or higher)
- Wide-brimmed hats
- Sunglasses with UV protection

5. First-Aid Kit

It's always a good idea to carry a small first-aid kit, especially when hiking or exploring the outdoors with kids. Include items like band-aids, antiseptic wipes, insect bite cream, and tweezers for splinters.

- **What to Include**: Don't forget personal medications your child might need, such as an inhaler, allergy medicine, or an EpiPen.

6. Entertainment for Travel

Long car rides through scenic drives like the **Icefields Parkway** or down-time at the hotel can be tough for kids. Bring along books, games, or tablets loaded with offline activities to keep them entertained during quiet moments.

Passes and Travel Documents for Kids

1. Park Passes

All visitors to Banff and Jasper National Parks need a valid park pass. Kids under 17 enter the parks for **free**, but you still need to get a pass for the adults in your group.

- **Where to Get Passes**: You can purchase park passes at entry gates, visitor centers, or online through the Parks Canada website.
- **Types of Passes**: If you're visiting multiple parks or staying for an extended period, consider the **Discovery Pass**, which gives unlimited access to all national parks for a year.

2. Identification and Documents

While you don't need a passport for kids traveling within Canada, it's a good idea to have some form of identification for each child, especially if flying into Calgary or Edmonton.

- **International Travelers**: If you're visiting from outside Canada, make sure your children have their passports, and check entry requirements depending on your country. The **Electronic Travel Authorization (eTA)** might be needed for some international travelers.

Safety Tips for Traveling with Kids

1. Stay Together and Keep a Watchful Eye

Whether hiking, exploring lakes, or walking through town, it's important to keep close to your kids. Outdoor settings like forests and rocky trails can be unpredictable, and children can wander off if not watched carefully.

- **Pro Tip**: For hikes or large open areas, consider giving each child a small whistle to use in case they get separated from the group.

2. Bear Safety

Banff and Jasper are bear country, so it's essential to follow all bear safety guidelines, even with kids. This includes keeping noise levels up while on trails to avoid startling wildlife, and teaching kids not to approach or feed animals. Carry bear spray (and know how to use it), and always store food properly while camping or picnicking.

- **What to Teach Kids**: Kids should learn to never run from a bear, stay calm, and follow instructions from adults in case of a wildlife sighting.

3. Emergency Contacts and Resources

Both Banff and Jasper have emergency services available in case of injury or a medical emergency. Make sure you have a fully charged phone with emergency numbers stored.

- **Important Contacts**:

Emergency Services: Dial **911** for immediate assistance.

Visitor Centers: Park rangers and staff are always available at visitor centers to provide help, answer questions, and give advice on trails and conditions.

Mobile Reception: Cell service can be unreliable in remote areas, so bring a physical map, especially if hiking in the backcountry.

Final Preparation Tips

- **Check Trail Conditions**: Before heading out, check with park rangers for up-to-date trail conditions. Some areas may be closed due to weather, wildlife activity, or maintenance.

- **Avoid Overpacking**: Kids may get tired of carrying too much, so pack light and use daypacks with essential items like snacks, water, and sunscreen. Encourage kids to help carry small items to make them feel involved.

- **Breaks and Rest**: Kids tire more easily than adults, so make sure to plan for breaks, especially during hikes. Choose family-friendly trails like **Johnston Canyon** in Banff or **Valley of the Five Lakes** in Jasper, which are manageable even for younger children.

Traveling with Your Pets in Banff and Jasper National Parks

Traveling with your pets to Banff and Jasper National Parks can be a rewarding experience, allowing your furry companions to explore the great outdoors alongside you. However, there are important guidelines and safety tips to ensure both your pets and the wildlife are protected. Here's a detailed guide on how to travel safely and responsibly with your pets in these parks, including pet-friendly accommodations, outdoor activities, and restrictions to be aware of.

Pet-Friendly Travel Guidelines

1. Pets Must Be Leashed at All Times

In both Banff and Jasper National Parks, it is mandatory to keep your pets on a leash no longer than 2 meters (6 feet) at all times, even when hiking or camping. This rule helps protect local wildlife and ensures the safety of your pet, as the parks are home to animals such as bears, elk, and coyotes, which can pose a danger if your pet roams freely.

- **Why It's Important**: Unleashed pets can trigger aggressive behavior from wildlife or may chase smaller animals. Keeping pets leashed reduces the risk of dangerous encounters and protects the fragile ecosystem.

2. Always Pick Up After Your Pet

Visitors are required to clean up after their pets in both Banff and Jasper. Carry waste bags and dispose of pet waste in designated trash bins to keep the parks clean and prevent the spread of disease to wildlife.

3. Do Not Leave Pets Unattended

Pets should not be left unattended in vehicles or campsites. Leaving pets in a vehicle, especially in the summer months, can lead to heatstroke, even with windows partially open. Always ensure your pet has access to water and shade.

Best Pet-Friendly Activities in Banff and Jasper

1. Pet-Friendly Hiking Trails

While not all trails are pet-friendly, many scenic routes allow leashed pets, making it possible to explore the beautiful outdoors with your dog.

- **Banff**:
- **Tunnel Mountain Trail**: This is a short and moderately easy hike near the town of Banff, making

it ideal for pets and families. The trail offers beautiful panoramic views of the Bow Valley and Banff.
- **Location**: Tunnel Mountain Rd, Banff, AB T1L 1E1

- **Fenland Trail**: This flat, forested loop trail near the town of Banff is perfect for an easy walk with your dog. It follows the banks of the Bow River and offers a peaceful setting.
- **Location**: Fenland Trailhead, Banff, AB.

Jasper:
- **Valley of the Five Lakes**: A relatively easy and popular trail, this hike takes you through forests and along a series of five stunning blue-green lakes. Dogs are welcome as long as they remain leashed.

Location: 9 kilometers south of Jasper townsite along Icefields Parkway.

Old Fort Point Trail: Another great option for hiking with your dog, this trail offers views of Jasper town and the surrounding mountains.

Location: Old Fort Point Rd, Jasper, AB.

2. Camping with Pets

Many campgrounds in Banff and Jasper are pet-friendly, as long as pets are kept on a leash and remain under control at all times. Some campgrounds have more open spaces, so be sure to choose one that suits your pet's needs.

- **Pet-Friendly Campgrounds**:

Tunnel Mountain Village Campgrounds (Banff): With spacious sites and easy access to pet-friendly hiking trails,

Tunnel Mountain is a great option for families traveling with pets.

- **Location**: 300 Tunnel Mountain Rd, Banff, AB.

Wapiti Campground (Jasper): Located close to Jasper townsite, this campground has scenic views of the Athabasca River and easy access to pet-friendly trails.

- **Location**: Highway 93A, Jasper, AB.

3. Pet-Friendly Boat Rentals

Some boat rental companies in Banff and Jasper allow pets on canoes or kayaks, making for a unique adventure on the water with your pet.

- **Canoe Rentals at Pyramid Lake (Jasper)**: Pets are allowed on rented canoes at **Pyramid Lake**, a serene spot perfect for paddling and relaxing with your dog. Just make sure your pet is comfortable in the boat and that you have a plan for safety.
  - **Location**: Pyramid Lake Rd, Jasper, AB.

4. Enjoying Scenic Drives

The **Icefields Parkway** is one of the most scenic drives in the world, connecting Banff and Jasper. With numerous pull-offs and picnic spots, it's a fantastic option for families with pets. While your pet must remain leashed at these stops, they can stretch their legs and take in the breathtaking surroundings.

Pet-Friendly Accommodations

Both Banff and Jasper offer a variety of pet-friendly hotels, lodges, and cabins that welcome your furry companions.

1. Fairmont Banff Springs

- **Location**: 405 Spray Ave, Banff, AB T1L 1J4
- **Pet Policy**: The iconic Fairmont Banff Springs welcomes pets and offers pet-friendly rooms with cozy bedding for your pet. The hotel provides bowls and treats, but there's an additional pet fee per night.
- **Tip**: The hotel is close to pet-friendly trails, such as **Tunnel Mountain**, making it convenient for outdoor adventures.

2. Jasper Park Lodge

- **Location**: Old Lodge Rd, Jasper, AB T0E 1E0
- **Pet Policy**: This luxury lodge is pet-friendly and offers amenities like dog beds and bowls upon request. Pets are welcome in designated rooms, and the property is surrounded by beautiful grounds for short walks with your pet.
- **Tip**: The nearby **Lac Beauvert Loop** is a perfect, easy trail for walking your dog along the scenic lake.

3. HI Banff Alpine Centre (Budget Option)

- **Location**: 801 Hidden Ridge Way, Banff, AB T1L 1B3

- **Pet Policy**: This budget-friendly hostel offers pet-friendly private rooms, making it a great option for travelers on a budget. It's located near several pet-friendly trails, including **Fenland Trail**.
- **Tip**: Book early, as their pet-friendly rooms are limited.

Important Considerations for Traveling with Pets.

1. Wildlife Awareness

Both Banff and Jasper are home to a variety of wildlife, including bears, wolves, and elk. It's important to be vigilant when traveling with your pet, as wildlife encounters can happen on trails or near campgrounds.

- **Safety Tip**: Keep your pet leashed at all times and avoid trails known for recent wildlife activity. Carry bear spray and be mindful of any wildlife advisories posted at trailheads or visitor centers.

2. Health and Comfort

Make sure your pet is healthy and up for the adventure. Bring plenty of water for your pet, especially if hiking on a hot day, and pack extra food. Pet-safe paw wax or booties can help protect their feet from hot pavement or rough terrain.

- **Tip**: Check with your vet before any major trip to ensure your pet is up to date on vaccinations and flea/tick prevention.

3. Pet Restrictions in Some Areas

While many outdoor areas are pet-friendly, some parts of the parks, such as backcountry trails and certain lakes, have restrictions on pets due to sensitive wildlife or environmental concerns. Always check in advance to avoid disappointment.

- **Examples of Pet-Restricted Areas**:
    - **Johnson Lake** (Banff) and **Cavell Meadows** (Jasper) are among the areas that may have pet restrictions.

Final Tips for Traveling with Pets

- **Know Your Pet's Limits**: Not all pets are used to the outdoors, so make sure to choose pet-friendly activities that suit their temperament and physical abilities. Gradual exposure to hikes and travel will ensure they enjoy the trip as much as you do.

- **Prepare for the Unexpected**: Always bring along extra water, food, and a blanket for your pet, as the weather in the Rockies can change quickly.

- **Follow the Rules**: Respect the local wildlife and environment by keeping your pet leashed, cleaning up after them, and being considerate of other visitors.

With proper planning and adherence to park regulations, traveling with your pet to Banff and Jasper can be a fantastic way to enjoy the great outdoors together!

Chapter 13

Photography Tips: Capturing the Beauty of the Parks

Alright, you're here to capture the stunning beauty of Banff and Jasper, and let me tell you, these parks offer some of the most breathtaking photography opportunities in the world. To make sure you get those postcard-worthy shots, timing and location are everything. Let's dive into some of the top spots and the best times of day to photograph them.

1. Lake Louise (Banff National Park)

Best Time to Photograph: Early morning or late evening.

Why? Lake Louise is one of the most iconic locations in Banff, with its emerald green water reflecting the surrounding peaks and the majestic Victoria Glacier. In the early morning, especially around sunrise, you'll catch the calm, glassy water reflecting the stunning landscape. The crowds are minimal, which means fewer interruptions and those first rays of sunlight will give the scene a warm, golden glow.

- **Morning**: You'll want to get there early, around **6:00 AM** in the summer, as the lake's surface is at its calmest. The early morning light brings out the best colors in the water and the sky.
- **Evening**: If you're there for sunset, the golden light hitting the glacier creates dramatic contrasts. This is ideal for capturing long-exposure shots of the lake's serene atmosphere.

2. Moraine Lake (Banff National Park)

Best Time to Photograph: Sunrise, hands down.

Why? Moraine Lake, with its vivid turquoise waters and the Ten Peaks towering in the background, is best captured during sunrise when the peaks catch the first light. The sun rises directly onto the Ten Peaks, making them glow with warm hues against the deep blue sky.

- **Morning (Sunrise)**: You'll want to arrive before **5:30 AM** to secure a good spot, as this is one of the most photographed lakes in the world. The early morning light creates stunning reflections in the water, and the lake is often calm, with fewer visitors around. In the early hours, the sky can take on a pinkish tone, which makes for a magical composition.

- **Afternoon**: If you miss sunrise, consider visiting around mid-afternoon for a different type of light, though the sun will be directly overhead, which can cause some harsh shadows.

3. Icefields Parkway

Best Time to Photograph: Mid-morning to late afternoon.

Why? The **Icefields Parkway** is a photographer's paradise, stretching from Banff to Jasper with towering mountains, turquoise lakes, and expansive glaciers. The lighting here can be tricky because of the elevation changes and the surrounding peaks, but mid-morning to late afternoon provides good contrast without being too harsh.

- **Morning**: Starting your drive early in the day, around **9:00 AM**, allows you to capture the sun illuminating the glaciers like the Athabasca Glacier without the harsh midday glare.
- **Late Afternoon**: Around **4:00 PM**, the sun will be lower in the sky, casting a warm light over the mountains. This is perfect for long-exposure shots of waterfalls like **Sunwapta Falls** and **Athabasca Falls**.

4. Peyto Lake (Banff National Park)

Best Time to Photograph: Early morning or late evening.

Why? The iconic wolf's-head-shaped **Peyto Lake** is best viewed from the overlook on the Icefields Parkway. This lake is known for its brilliant turquoise color, which is caused by the glacier rock flour suspended in the water.

- **Morning**: Arrive by **7:00 AM** for an undisturbed view with soft lighting. In the early morning, the lake's color is at its richest, and the lack of crowds lets you capture the whole scene with the dramatic peaks in the background.

- **Evening**: Just before sunset, the lake catches the last light of the day, providing a softer glow on the surrounding peaks. The evening is also ideal if you're looking for a quieter experience'

5. Spirit Island, Maligne Lake (Jasper National Park)

Best Time to Photograph: Mid-morning or late afternoon.

Why? The iconic **Spirit Island** in **Maligne Lake** is only accessible by boat, so timing is essential for getting the best photos. Mid-morning offers some of the clearest reflections on the lake.

- **Morning**: If you're taking a boat tour, aim for one departing between **9:00 AM** and **11:00 AM**. At this time, the sun is positioned perfectly to illuminate **Spirit Island** and the surrounding peaks, giving you balanced lighting without harsh shadows.

- **Afternoon**: The golden hour around **4:00 PM** to **5:00 PM** creates stunning contrasts between the island and the surrounding mountains, especially in the fall, when the larches turn a brilliant yellow.

6. Athabasca Glacier (Jasper National Park)

Best Time to Photograph: Late morning to early afternoon.

Why? **Athabasca Glacier** is one of the largest and most accessible glaciers in North America. Due to its elevation and the reflective surface of the ice, photographing the glacier works best when the sun is high enough to provide good lighting without too many shadows.

- **Mid-morning to Early Afternoon**: Between **10:00 AM and 2:00 PM**, you can capture the glacier's sheer size with the best natural light. The blue tones of the ice stand out during this time, especially if the sky is clear.

7. Bow Lake (Banff National Park)

Best Time to Photograph: Sunrise or sunset.

Why? Bow Lake is one of the largest lakes in Banff and offers stunning reflections of the surrounding peaks and glaciers. The lake is especially photogenic at sunrise or sunset when the water is calm, and the light is soft.

- **Morning (Sunrise)**: Around **5:00 AM to 6:00 AM** in the summer, the rising sun casts a warm glow on the water, perfectly reflecting **Bow Glacier** and the surrounding mountains. It's peaceful and quiet, giving you time to get the perfect shot.

- **Evening (Sunset)**: Bow Lake is also ideal for sunset shots, with the colors of the sky reflecting off the glassy water. Aim for **8:00 PM** during summer for the golden hour magic.

General Photography Tips for Banff and Jasper

- **Use a Tripod**: For low-light situations, such as sunrise or sunset, using a tripod will help you capture sharper images, especially for long exposures of waterfalls or night photography.

- **Filters**: A polarizing filter can help reduce glare from the water and bring out the vibrant colors of lakes like Moraine or Peyto. A neutral density filter is perfect for long-exposure shots of moving water.

- **Timing is Everything**: Arriving early (before sunrise) or staying late (around sunset) will not only give you the best light but also help avoid the crowds, especially at popular spots like Lake Louise and Moraine Lake.

With these tips, you'll be well on your way to capturing the raw beauty of Banff and Jasper like a pro. The combination of pristine landscapes and optimal lighting will make your photos stand out, whether you're photographing the famous turquoise lakes, towering glaciers, or dramatic mountain peaks.

Photography Etiquette to Protect Nature and Other Visitors

While taking photographs, it's important to respect the environment and fellow travelers. Here are some key etiquette tips:

1. Stay on Marked Trails

- **Why**: Venturing off marked trails can damage fragile ecosystems, trample vegetation, and disturb wildlife habitats. Stay on designated paths to protect the environment and reduce your impact.

2. Maintain a Safe Distance from Wildlife

- **Why**: It's essential to respect wildlife and maintain a safe distance. Parks Canada recommends keeping at least 30 meters (100 feet) from larger animals like elk and 100 meters (300 feet) from bears. Using a telephoto lens allows you to capture animals without approaching them.

3. Avoid Flash Photography with Wildlife

- **Why**: Flash can startle animals, causing them unnecessary stress or agitation. When photographing wildlife, use natural light or increase your ISO to brighten the image without needing a flash.

4. Don't Block Scenic Viewpoints

- **Why**: Popular spots like Lake Louise or Moraine Lake can get crowded, especially at sunrise or sunset. Be considerate of other visitors by stepping aside once you've taken your shot. Avoid setting up tripods in narrow spaces where others are trying to enjoy the view.

5. Leave No Trace

- **Why**: Always carry out what you bring in. Don't leave any litter, food, or items behind at your photo spots. This helps preserve the pristine beauty of the parks for others and protects the wildlife from potential hazards.

Chapter 14

Final Tips for a Memorable Trip

When visiting Banff and Jasper, practicing eco-friendly travel and adhering to Leave No Trace principles can help preserve the pristine beauty of these parks for future generations. Here are some key tips to ensure a memorable and sustainable trip:

1. Plan Ahead and Prepare

Planning ahead is one of the core principles of eco-friendly travel. By organizing your trip carefully, you can minimize your environmental impact.

- **Research Park Rules**: Familiarize yourself with the guidelines for camping, hiking, and wildlife safety in both Banff and Jasper. Respect seasonal closures and stay updated on any trail restrictions to protect sensitive areas.

- **Stay on Designated Trails**: Sticking to marked paths minimizes harm to fragile ecosystems and prevents soil erosion. Avoid creating your own trails, as this can damage vegetation and disturb wildlife habitats,

2. Pack Eco-Friendly Supplies

What you bring with you can make a significant difference in reducing waste and protecting the environment.

- **Reusable Gear**: Bring a reusable water bottle, utensils, and containers to avoid single-use plastics. Both Banff and Jasper have plenty of spots to refill water bottles, such as visitor centers or restaurants.
- **Eco-Friendly Toiletries**: Use biodegradable soaps and shampoos if you plan to camp, and make sure to dispose of any waste responsibly.

3. Leave No Trace

The **Leave No Trace** principles are essential to preserving the natural beauty of the parks.

- **Carry Out What You Carry In**: Take all your trash with you, even food scraps. Organic matter like fruit peels may take years to decompose in high-altitude environments and can attract wildlife, leading to dangerous encounters.
- **Respect Wildlife**: Avoid feeding or approaching animals. Feeding wildlife can alter their natural behaviors, making them dependent on human food and putting both the animals and visitors at risk.

Observe animals from a distance using a zoom lens or binoculars.

4. Choose Sustainable Transportation

Reducing your carbon footprint can be as simple as choosing eco-friendly transportation.

- **Shuttle Services and Public Transit**: Both Banff and Jasper offer shuttle services to popular attractions like Lake Louise and Moraine Lake. These reduce vehicle traffic and help protect the environment by cutting down on carbon emissions.
- **Carpool or Rent Hybrid Vehicles**: If driving is necessary, consider carpooling with friends or renting a hybrid or electric vehicle. You can also reduce fuel consumption by planning efficient routes and driving at eco-friendly speeds.

5. Respect Local Flora and Fauna

- **Do Not Pick Plants**: The unique flora in the Canadian Rockies is delicate and slow-growing due to the high altitude. Admire wildflowers and plants but leave them undisturbed for others to enjoy.
- **Use Bear-Proof Containers**: When camping, always store food in bear-proof containers or in your vehicle to prevent attracting wildlife to your campsite. This reduces dangerous encounters and keeps both you and the animals safe'

6. Support Local and Sustainable Businesses

When dining or shopping in Banff and Jasper, choose businesses that prioritize sustainability.

- **Buy Local Products**: Support local artisans, shops, and farmers' markets, which help reduce transportation emissions and support the local economy.
- **Eat Sustainably**: Look for restaurants that offer locally sourced, sustainable food options. Many restaurants in Banff and Jasper emphasize farm-to-table menus and eco-conscious practices.

7. Conserve Water and Energy

Even though Banff and Jasper are located near abundant natural water sources, it's still important to conserve resources.

- **Minimize Water Use**: Take shorter showers and turn off taps when brushing your teeth. If you're camping, use biodegradable soap and wash away from natural water sources to prevent contamination.
- **Energy Conservation**: Turn off lights and heating in your accommodation when not in use. If camping, use solar-powered chargers for your devices.

By following these tips, you can enjoy your adventure in Banff and Jasper while leaving a positive impact on the environment. Practicing eco-friendly travel helps preserve the parks' natural beauty, ensuring that future visitors will experience the same awe-inspiring landscapes.

Insider Tips from Locals and Park Rangers

Here's how to enhance your trip to Banff and Jasper, with insider tips and a list of must-do activities for an unforgettable experience.

Local Insider Tips for Banff and Jasper

1. Visit During Shoulder Seasons (Spring and Fall)

If you want to avoid the crowds and experience Banff and Jasper more peacefully, plan your visit during the shoulder seasons in **May-June** or **September-October**. During these months, the parks are quieter, accommodation rates tend to be lower, and you still get beautiful weather with less traffic on popular trails like **Johnston Canyon** and at iconic spots like **Moraine Lake**.

- **Tip**: In the fall, the **Larch Valley** near Moraine Lake turns a stunning golden color, making it one of the most scenic and less crowded hikes.

2. Early Mornings for Popular Spots

If you're visiting during the summer, head to the major attractions like **Lake Louise, Moraine Lake**, and **Peyto Lake** as early as possible—think **before 7:00 AM**. You'll avoid crowds and get the best lighting for photography. By midday, these places can be packed, especially during July and August.

- **Tip**: For **Moraine Lake**, the parking lot fills up very early, so either arrive before sunrise or take the shuttle service that runs from Lake Louise during peak season.

3. Stargazing in Jasper (Dark Sky Preserve)

Jasper is known for its **Dark Sky Preserve**, meaning it has minimal light pollution and offers incredible stargazing opportunities. The best places to view the night sky include **Pyramid Lake**, **Maligne Lake**, and **Old Fort Point**. The Jasper Dark Sky Festival in October is also a great time to visit for astrophotography and to experience expert talks on astronomy.

- **Tip**: Head out for stargazing after 10:00 PM in the summer, and if you're visiting in autumn, you might even catch a glimpse of the **Northern Lights**.

4. Take Scenic Routes

While the Icefields Parkway is one of the most famous scenic drives, don't forget smaller routes like the **Bow Valley Parkway**. This drive between Banff and Lake Louise is less crowded and offers excellent chances to see wildlife such as elk or bears, especially early in the morning or late in the day.

- **Tip**: Stop at **Johnston Canyon** on the Bow Valley Parkway for an easy, family-friendly hike through a stunning canyon with waterfalls.

5. Book in Advance

If you're planning to stay at popular accommodations like the **Fairmont Chateau Lake Louise** or want to do special activities such as the **Glacier Adventure Tour**, book early—especially for visits during the summer months. These fill up quickly due to the high demand, and last-minute bookings can be challenging.

- **Tip**: Even activities like **canoe rentals** at Moraine Lake and **Maligne Lake Cruises** should be reserved in advance to guarantee availability.

Acknowledgement

Dear Reader,

Thank you for choosing this guidebook to help plan your visit to **Canadian Rockies, Banff & Jasper**. I hope my experiences and insights provide valuable information to enhance your trip and make it truly memorable.

Please note that while every effort has been made to ensure the accuracy of the information in this guide, tourist services and attractions can change over time. Therefore, I encourage you to check the latest details online before embarking on your journey.

Wishing you safe travels and an unforgettable adventure in the beautiful **Canadian Rockies.**

Best regards,

Miles B. Carter.

Disclaimer

This guidebook contains valuable information and recommendations for travelers. However, please be aware that services, attractions, and details mentioned may change over time. It is advisable to verify the current status of attractions, accommodations, and services through reliable online sources before your trip. The author and publisher are not responsible for any changes or discrepancies in the information provided.

Safe travels and enjoy your time in **Canadian Rockies**!

Travel Planners & Maps.

You can use your phone to scan QR code to view BANFF map.

You can use your phone to scan QR code to view Jasper Map.

Planner

TRAVEL PLANNER
FOR BANFF

DESTINATION DURATION:

MUST VISIT PLACES
-
-
-
-

FOODS TO TRY

DAY 1

DAY 2

DAY 3

BUDGET

HOW DID TODAY GO?

TRAVEL PLANNER
FOR JASPER

DESTINATION					DURATION:

MUST VISIT PLACES
-
-
-
-

FOODS TO TRY

DAY 1

DAY 2

DAY 3

BUDGET

HOW DID TODAY GO?

Printed in Great Britain
by Amazon